STOP THOUGHT
Proven Methods For Deep
Meditation & Enlightenment
2024 ©
Author: Michele Blood

Published by Michele's MusiVation Int'l
PO Box 12933
La Jolla, California 92037
USA
All rights reserved.
Printed in the United States of America
ISBN: 978-1-890679-65-1

This book may not be copied, duplicated or used in any way without the written permission of the publishers.

For wholesale copies
email team@TheMysticalExperience.com

Cover art by Johnny Endara

Dedication

To The Great, Enlightened Teacher
Kundalini
Thank you Forever.

A Huge thank you to Our Mystical Team
Holly Fallah, Treavor Rogers & Johnny Endara

The Most Beautiful, Wise Souls I Have
The Privilege To Create With Every Day.
GO, MYSTICAL TEAM!

Table Of Contents

Foreword From A Student	i
Instructions	iii
Talks On Meditation Techniques	4
A Story Of Enlightenment	5
Starting The Practice	9
Affirmations	25
How To Become A Conduit For The Light	38
Meditating To Music	45
Spiritual Anatomy	55
Third Eye Chakra Meditation	67
Heart Chakra Meditation	76
Pathways To Enlightenment	82
Which Spiritual Aspirant Are You?	93
Bhakti Yoga	103
Kriya Yoga	112
Silent Meditation	119
The Stargate	126
Mala Beads	132
Gazing Meditation	141
Bells And Singing Bowls	146
Candles	151
Mudras	156
Laughing	173
Diet And Exercise	180

Table Of Contents

Praying For Others Raises Consciousness	188
What Is Prayer	194
Simple Prayers To Uplift Loved Ones	204
Mindfulness	211
Resources	221

Foreword From A Student

Like most people, I have heard the word *Enlightenment* before. For me, it was in my college Zen Buddhism class, where I learned about old, bald men who once, long ago, were Enlightened, and were above life and death. They had escaped the wheel of *Samsara*, and their suffering was over. This sounded very mythical to me. It also sounded historical, like this was something that took place long ago.

So, you could see my bewilderment and surprise when a friend of mine told me about this woman who was Enlightened. *No! Could it be? I thought that only happened to old, bald Buddhist men hundreds of years ago,* I thought. I understood the rarity and gravity of this word, and how few people in my Zen Buddhism history books were able to achieve this.

But it wasn't until I joined my first group call with this Enlightened Teacher that I got to experience it for myself. She seemed like a very normal person, who did normal things, like cooking or taking care of her cats. She had a vibrant and enthusiastic personality, and I could feel that she loved everyone on the call. Then she did some things that were not so normal, like Meditation and Transmitting Light. I didn't really know what this all meant at the time, however, I did feel so good after these calls, and just alive.

I started meditation practice, which at first felt like a lot of nothing. Then, after about a month I felt that Electric, Divine Current in my brain, which She mentioned is what this Light is that She is transmitting. I was happy and in awe to be experiencing something like that.

I have been with my Teacher for many years now, and I can say that She is the person I always knew existed. I had always wondered if there was just one person out there who was 100% selfless. I just felt that there had to be. And recently at a live event of Hers, I 100% knew what Love was. True, Pure, Real, Selfless Love. I was graced with this experience and I will never forget it. In awe of the Beauty of this Light flowing from Her, I wanted not a thing from Her, not even Enlightenment, but only to Serve and Love this lady of Light. And this Light is everywhere and is in all of us.

Through this Light, the world is awakening one person at a time, showing us that Enlightenment is not just a historical concept but a living, breathing reality that is possible for everyone in this very lifetime.

The pages that follow are transcripts I put together from her live and Zoom events. What is amazing is Michele never prepares a talk, it just flows out from her.

I know Michele always acknowledged her Enlightened Teacher, Kundalini, because as Michele says none of this would be possible without this Magnificent soul. Thank you, Kundalini.

Foreword by Holly Fallah, student.

Instructions

Enjoy this book, and may you also discover your own inner power, potential and Enlightenment.

We have added some blank pages after each topic to allow you to write down your experiences, satori moments (what the world calls aha! moments) and realizations.

Writing down the messages you feel true synergy with will give you clarity and higher consciousness.

I AM with you during your experience with this book and know that you are never alone and that you are truly loved.

ALL Things Are Possible For You, My Dearest.

In Love and Oneness,
Michele

Talks On Meditation Techniques

Please enjoy these live talks from Michele on Meditation Practice Techniques that will lead you to Deeper States of Meditation, and eventual Enlightenment.

Introduction From A Live Event
A Story Of Enlightenment
From A Live Zoom Event

The Purpose Of Life Is Enlightenment

Hello, this is Michele Blood and I have been teaching manifestation, visualization, meditation, and affirmation music for over 30 years. I have worked with the late, great Bob Proctor. We co-created many positive seminars, products and books together over many years. I've shared the stage internationally with Dr. Deepak Chopra, Dr. Wayne Dyer, Louise Hay, and many other great people. I've been doing this for a long time.

I started as a musician, as a rock singer in Australia, and after a near-fatal car accident in 1987, I had a life-changing epiphany of doing affirmations with music to heal my body. These Affirmation Songs not only healed my body when I was in the hospital but also created great, worldwide success. I was making great money, singing, speaking all over the world, living in Malaysia, and running Bob Proctor's company in Asia. I knew how to, what the world calls, *manifest*. I knew how to co-create, but I knew it was always the Divine. My love for the Divine was so much more important to me than materialistic things. It's good to have confidence in the Divine and to be connected so that you can use your will and your intention. Beautiful experiences and material wealth manifested, however I wanted to go deeper to really know my own Divine Presence.

My heart was out there, glowing, and I thought it was just normal to have this sort of *heart glow*, as I used to call it. I went to so many different countries looking for someone who knew God. I didn't really know what

Enlightenment was. I'd heard of it, but I knew it was perhaps a Buddhist saying. I knew I was looking for someone who knew God. I was brought up as a Catholic, and I actually had a wonderful experience growing up as a Catholic. I was with beautiful Irish nuns and lived in the countryside in the blue mountains of Australia. It was wonderful. As a child, I was in love with Jesus and went to as many masses daily with the nuns as my Mum would allow.

As a young adult, I realized that my happiness was to find God. I knew that to find God, I would have to find someone who knew God. Later I realized that that is what Enlightenment is. So, I went to many, many different countries. I lived in Malaysia for a while, and I worked with the great, wonderful soul Bob Proctor, Dr. Deepak Chopra, Dr. Wayne Dyer, and Louise Hay. I was a speaker and a singer and travelled the world working with all these great speakers. It was wonderful.

However, it wasn't enough. These people were wonderful and some of them were very in love with the light, with God. However, they didn't know God. I could feel that they didn't. They had a love for God, but I wanted someone who had a union with God, an actual union. So, I was exceptionally blessed to meet an Enlightened Teacher. I had searched the globe for over 12 years, and I finally met my Teacher, Kundalini, when I walked into an event she had in San Diego. And thank God the Spirit guided me to come to America because there she was. I had seen gurus and different people from all over the world, and I had sat in front of a couple of Indian gurus who were Enlightened. But it wasn't for me. It didn't quite fit. Maybe because it was a different language and culture. Both didn't even speak English. I don't know what it was, but it still wasn't for me. So, I did find a couple of people who had that conscious union with God, called Enlightenment, called a Kundalini Awakening, whatever you choose to call it.

But my Enlightened Teacher was a Western woman; a beautiful, young woman. And when she put her hands up, I saw Light glowing out of her hands. I was looking around to see if anyone else saw that. My eyes were watering up, and I was dazed and blissed out. *What is going on here?*, I thought. After all those years of searching to find God, I realized that all that light that she was transmitting was what had been missing from my path. I had to find that person who was in union with God. And in this beautiful form; funny, outrageous sometimes, so loving, so strong, and powerful. But I would always be blown away and think, *How is there so much Light coming through this small woman?* Before I started understanding it, it would just blow my mind. It kept blowing my mind, thank God. Her name is Kundalini. A Perfect Spiritual name for this amazing and young woman at least 10 years younger than me.

I was so blessed that she agreed to be my Teacher. And so, I did everything that she said to do. And I could feel when I was practicing my meditation, that Light coming through me. I could feel tingling at the top of my head, and I was feeling an even stronger heart glow. I didn't realize it at the time, but the reason I had a heart glow was because my heart chakra had already been partially activated from past lives and I was born that way. So, meeting her and having this Light transmitted, I could really meditate deeply.

Being able to tap into someone's consciousness who is in union with God is the fast road. And it wasn't always easy, but it was worth it a million times over.

The ego can become very, very confounded and agitated. *What is going on here? I don't want to die.* Eventually, I started having what I call Stargate experiences where I would just take off. Bees would be buzzing in my head, there were huge sounds, and then I'd be flying through this Stargate, just like the TV show. I'd be off into these different dimensions until eventually one day, one blessed day, the Kundalini completely went out of my Sushumna, my crown chakra, and everything exploded into Light. It's all so simple. But it would never have happened without that amazing, amazing Teacher, Kundalini.

This had happened to me as a child a few times, however I was so young I did not understand what it was. I remember I told my Mum I was flying through space. And she would say oh what a fun dream, however, I was not dreaming.

Starting The Practice

The Practice Of Meditation Is A Privilege

Meditation practice, what a beautiful thing. Not always easy. If meditation practice was easy, everyone in the world would do it. Because the benefits that you gain, and the incredible experiences that you end up having from meditation practice, make you healthier and more peaceful. Silencing all those weird thoughts makes you stronger, calmer, and more powerful within. You have more confidence in your spirit and are more loving, compassionate, and kind, and it just feels so good.

When you have other things to do, you become happier and say, *Oh wow, just two more hours and I get to meditate.* It's like when you were younger, or whenever you had to go and meet a lover. It's like, *Two hours to go and now, oh my God, I get to go and meditate. Oh yay.* Where time stands still, or that illusion called time is gone, all fear also disappears, and life is a beautiful song.

Is everyone listening and paying attention? Great. So, let's get to the basics of meditation practice. I feel it is so powerfully important that your spirit is cleansed for this special practice. Clean the area where you practice your meditation, no matter where it is, it's important that it's clean. One of the wonderful ways to keep it clean is just through natural spring water. Put a whole lot of love into that water. You can put the words Love, Adore You God, whatever you want on that water first. The water responds immediately to love, and you just wash down that area with the water.

If the area has carpet, vacuum. Wash down the walls around the area with that water, and then you can burn some incense around that area. You can use a little bit of Nag Champa incense. You don't have to smoke the whole place out, just a little bit to cleanse it. Going and searching for the right meditation mat is so much fun. Some people prefer a cushion. I use a cushion about four inches high, and that way you can sit comfortably in the lotus or half-lotus position to have your spine straight. If you have a challenge sitting up with your spine straight, there are special back braces for meditation that you can purchase. My friend Lawrence, who's quite tall, always had a challenge. He started doing a lot of exercise, yoga, and had a back brace as well so that he could keep his spine straight. Or you can sit in a comfortable chair and have a meditation cushion behind you to keep your spine straight, if that's a challenge.

A meditation chair is okay as long as you feel safe and know that if you fall over you're going to be safe, and you're not going to hit your head on something. Because eventually, you can be in such a still state of mind and not in your body that you do fall over. Trust me, it happens like, *Whoa, where am I now? Okay, get back on the mat.* This is a good thing because you've gone away. Thought has at last stopped.

I have found that the stronger my body becomes through exercise, the longer I've been able to sit up straight. Planks help a lot. As Kundalini always said to us, *You have got to do your sit-ups and push-ups.* And Kundalini has a black belt in Karate so she knows how good it is to be disciplined and always would remind us to exercise. Strengthening your spine assists to keep your core strong. If you have too much tummy fat, that isn't good for the back, so it's a good idea to release some of that tummy fat if you've got too much. I'm not talking about being skinny, I'm just saying that too much tummy fat weakens the spine because there's too much weight moving it forward. Walking for an hour every day will also give you stronger abs, and even if there's a little bit of tummy fat, that's fine. But having those strong abs is important for those who really want to be able to sit up straight.

All those pictures of the big fat Buddha, that wasn't really the Buddha, he was very, very slim. Those are just depictions of the prosperity pretend Buddha where if you rub his tummy, it's good luck. That's not what the Buddha looked like, that's for sure. And it doesn't mean that you can't have body fat. I'm just saying it's good to have strong abs even if it's underneath the fat. I have one Pilates teacher who's definitely not slim, but boy is she strong. I know underneath that tummy there's abs of steel, which is what it's all about, having strength.

Once you've got your little meditation area that you've chosen, whether you have a mat there or a chair, make sure that no one else sits there. This is your area, because every time you go back and sit there more and more Shakti, more and more Kundalini, more and more high vibration builds up in that area. And when you're practicing your meditation, the Light that is transmitted to you is more easily absorbed into your consciousness. You want a nice, clean area. If it's possible to have just a room that is just your meditation room, well that is wonderful as well. But say you can't. Say you share a place with people, well then just make sure you put your meditation mat away. Maybe put a towel down where you're going to put your meditation mat so that no one's sitting on your meditation mat.

It's nice to have some flowers there, or some sort of nature. If you can't have nature there, then light a candle. I always love lighting candles. It really does bring in the Light. It's a Mystical thing that some people don't believe in, but I know it works. I've seen it.

We don't ever meditate on our lower chakras. You have this Kundalini at the base of your spine. This is the high blessing of being a human, of being born a human. You are born with this nectar of the ether of the Divine Blood that is sitting at the base of your spine. This beautiful, clear tube is called the Sushumna.

It is along the base of the spine's ethereal tube. And it's blocked. It's blocked, so you can't feel the Divine Presence within you. Your intuition isn't strong because it's blocked. So, your chakras are aligned along this beautiful Sushumna and you can't feel the Divine through you because the Sushumna is blocked. Maybe once occasionally whenever you feel some love, but then it ends up having attachment to it because the Sushumna is blocked, and those chakras are not activated.

The reason we don't meditate on the lower chakras is, say the Kundalini starts becoming activated and starts coming up the Sushumna, but only to the level of those lower chakras. What happens then? You are in a state of horniness and insecurity. You can't feel satisfied with the world. You're in the lower chakra world, and the maya, the lower consciousness, can really affect you there. So, that's why we don't focus there. We focus first on the heart chakra, which is located along the spine, literally parallel to where you think it is in the front of your chest because you can feel it there. Eventually, you feel it along the Sushumna, you feel it where it is. And once that's activated, that means that the Kundalini, that Shakti, has come up and cleared the way. All of the other chakras then do become activated, but in a way that's going to give you balance and not put you out of whack with the world and feel like, *Oh, the postman looks handsome today.*

Awakening the Kundalini activates the chakras. It is vibrating bubbles of Light that I have seen, and it is miraculous how that vibration is scrubbing all the gunk away. And you go into those Divine Dimensions that are just literally not in this world. You get to experience beautiful beings of Light and waves of ecstasy. The bliss, when that's activated, even if it's just partially activated, is incredible. You can end up feeling your actual physical heart in any part of the body you focus on, your big toe, your little finger, anywhere, it's like everything's become activated.
Just as our Beloved Teacher, Kundalini, meditated for all of her students and transmitted this High, Vibratory Light, I now do this also for you guys. It is simply that I am used by the Light. I love to gaze each of your pictures and witness the Divine in you until the picture fades into Light and disappears. Then I pray for you and hug that picture and bow to the Divine in each of

you. Eventually, you start feeling those electrical currents through your brain, little tingles to start with, maybe itching of the scalp, or just hot pinpricks. Some of you I know have told me you felt it immediately and others it takes a little longer. However, even if you do not feel it straight away the Light is still working for you. It's activating parts of the brain.

Please do not meditate on the crown chakra. That is an act of grace that happens. I recommend that you meditate on your heart chakra in the evening. And then you meditate on your third eye, that is between your eyebrows and a little above, in the mornings, because that will help you stay focused and balanced. And we do want that to be activated as well. Men find that their third eye activates faster than their heart chakra because they've been brought up through their DNA to be strong and have a wall. It's a totally unconscious thing. Some men don't usually want their heart chakra to be activated too much. Too many feelings and emotions for a few men. Of course, none of you guys here today.

But I say to the men, if your third eye is more activated than your heart chakra, please for a month just meditate upon your heart chakra because you must have the Kundalini come up there. Otherwise, it's like a pseudo-activation. It hasn't enticed all the other chakras to be activated. It's just a partial activation. But you want that Kundalini to come up because eventually what happens is you go away after you are practicing and focusing on that chakra. You go away and you just feel yourself blend into the cosmos. And then, of course, you don't have to focus on that chakra at that point. It's just when you've had Light coming through your consciousness, then that Light that is sent to you will help focus your attention to that particular chakra to help it become activated.

The natural evolution of mankind is to become self-realized, to become Awakened, to become this beautiful Spiritual Being. There are no accidents. God didn't give you all those nerves and that huge brain for 3% to 10% of it to be used. It's all supposed to be activated. It activates different dimensions, different meridians, whatever you want to call the tiny chakras in the body that awaken until your body becomes a body of Light. People eventually can see it, but it's very, very hard to see that Light unless someone is already in a higher state of evolution.

It's a beautiful feeling when you find someone that you know you can trust, who can really send that Light to you, who's plugged in, and then can help you plug into your Divine Presence and help awaken those chakras. I meditated for many, many years, did affirmations, and many different things before I met my Beloved Teacher. I had many amazing, spiritual experiences, and I could always read a person, and see who they really were without judgement. My heart chakra was semi-activated. I was just this swoon of love for God, looking for God everywhere. And I used to say to people, *Can't you feel it? It's like a heart glow, like my heart's out of my chest.* And they're like *Are you in love?* I said, *Yes, with God. And I think it's here right now, but I'm not sure. I must find a Teacher to show me.* And remember I travelled all over the world for 14 years before I found Kundalini or She found me.

I had to find someone who loves God or who is self-realized. I didn't really understand what that was all about. I really searched for God in many different religions. I was so surprised because I thought if someone was in a religious order, that it was just a given that they were in love with God and that's all they wanted to talk about. But they'd want to talk about all this other stuff. And I'd say to myself, *No, no, no, no. Tell me about your prayer practice. Do you meditate? Do you do what Saint Teresa did to go into silent contemplation?* They'd be talking about something else. *I don't need to know what your way of life is or what you have for breakfast, honey. I want to know about a True, Mystical Union, I have to know God NOW!*

In the mornings, depending on your line of work, meditate on your third eye. When you know that you're finished for the day and you can get some sleep, well then meditate on your heart chakra and you'll go into that beautiful, blissful state as you're sleeping and be open and receptive to allow all this Light to enter your being. And it works so beautifully.

I remember my Teacher said she had this big job, and she said she could not go throughout the day without meditating at least once during the day as well. She would go to a little church that was nearby or she'd just go and bring her iPod with her music and meditate on the toilet.

I totally believe in Kriya Yoga breathing. It helps to still the mind so beautifully. If you find it hard to breathe through both nostrils, use a natural, organic, saline nasal spray. Do those three times a day and that eventually gets rid of allergies and different problems with your nose as well, but it also helps your breathing.

Please go to the link below for a video where I go through the steps for Kriya Yoga breathing.
https://www.TheMysticalExperience.com/KriyaYoga

Where you sleep is important. Get a nice, new pillow every few months. I like to sleep with a silk pillowcase that feels so fresh and beautiful. And if you cannot buy a new pillow, at least wash the one you have with very, very hot water in your washing machine with a tiny little bit of bleach and then wash it again to get rid of the bleach. And then a little bit of natural fabric softener as well. And if you've got a dryer, make sure it is really dry until it's bone dry, and that will help definitely clean it. You can add a little bit of purified water to the last rinse cycle. Make sure that you have your bedroom where you sleep really, really clean. Have beautiful pictures of Enlightened ones around your room. Saturate yourself in that Light.

I want you to all remember that you are not living a life of fate. That's not the Truth. There's no such thing as fate. Who makes your destiny? You do. Yes, the Divine has given you free will, an independence to shut out that beautiful power of Light, or to let it in. Your destiny will end up karmically. In other words, you'll be karmically thrown around the waves if you just live like the rest of the world, where all the past things you've done in this life and past lives, all your feelings and emotions that have stuck to the past, will just throw you around like the winds of the gust because they're not melted away yet by the clear Light of reality. You just don't know where you're going. The wind changes this way, that way, and you are just lost. You don't even realize it. So, that's what happens. You can allow your destiny to be God knows what, but that's your free will deciding, right? Or you can allow that Divine power in. You allow that Divine power in, and you make decisions on what it is that you want to achieve in your life. Not based on ego, but based on what you will achieve to live a happy, rich, fulfilling life. When you allow this Divine Light in, you're open and receptive to it. You have so much more power, so much more inner strength to overcome any difficulty, and any bit of trouble can be overcome.

Sometimes we do miss the mark, but we can remedy that because the Divine has given us reason and will. So, first you make a decision, correct? And I've spoken to some of you over the time I've known you, and suddenly one of you will say, *That's it. I've made a decision. I'm going to go for it now. I'm going to meditate. I'm really going to do it every day consistently. I'm going to give this thing a real go and see what happens. I've got nothing to lose and everything to gain.* And that's what happened to me a few months after meeting my Teacher where I was only meditating 30 minutes in the morning and only 30 minutes at night. One day I made the decision to go for it. And I didn't watch any movies. My television was thrown out. I didn't have the internet at home. I had to go to my office to be able to get on email.

I just said, *That's it. When I'm home, I meditate or I exercise. That's all I do. And I don't see anyone.* I didn't socialize. My transformation from that point on was so fast, my meditations went deeper and deeper. I still had challenges with the thoughts coming in, but I was determined, even if I had to meditate for quite a while, to have just that one moment of no thought. And having a flash of Light, even for a moment, was worth it, because I felt so ecstatic afterwards and so fulfilled within myself. I watched the movies that my Teacher recommended as homework assignments, but otherwise, I would just read spiritual books. I'd make a cup of tea, I'd meditate, I'd exercise, I'd go back to meditating, have a little bit of sleep, go to the office, meditate first in the morning, get up earlier so that I could do it for at least 2 hours.

And it took willpower and discipline. And we have a member that is a parent with two young daughters that he's bringing up on his own, and he's got a big full-time job. And he just decided to get up at four in the morning. He had to get up early to be able to meditate every morning. Now it's like a dream for him when he has a weekend off on his own, he can meditate all weekend. Yay.

Because it's exquisite. I mean no orgasm any of you guys have ever had will ever come close to the true bliss of meditation. And when you go beyond the bliss into just being absorbed in it, becoming that Light, it is beyond anything. You are not some floaty little fluff of bliss. That is not what I mean when I say blissful, it is Powerful and there is strength that comes through you. You must be strong actually to handle it. You are not the same ever again. Your body becomes a body of Light. This is natural evolution. Evolution of mankind, womankind.

However, this world is very tricky. There are so many different people in different states of mind, and in different stages of consciousness. We don't judge that. We've all been there, done that. We've all been arseholes at some stage, right? Yes. You've all been an arsehole at some stage. There's no saints here, right? In your past, okay, maybe someone doesn't agree with me. Does anyone here think that they've never been an arsehole in their entire life? Maybe you've thought an unkind thought or have been judgmental of yourself or someone else. You know what I mean?

As our Teacher, Kundalini, used to say, *Meditation Rocks.* Make up your mind to hold steady, using your willpower, to be consistent with your meditation. Even if you haven't been consistent, make up your mind that no matter what, you are going to practice meditation every morning and every evening, even if it's only for 15 minutes or 30 minutes out of 24 hours. That can change your life. Even after a week of just doing it consistently, you will be like, *Wow, I feel different. I feel good. I feel strong and focused. Wow, Meditation Really Does Rock.*

Sometimes you have to use your willpower. When you want to release weight, eventually you're not attracted to cakes and chocolate because you're so used to not eating them. You're so used to eating Prana food. It would just be ridiculous for you to eat a piece of chocolate. It's just the same as that. You're disciplining yourself to awaken those spiritual powers and to claim your Divinity so you can become one. You are uniting your consciousness with God, and you receive blessings and blessings and blessings this way. The Divine wants you to have everything. Mother Meera says that, and boy is she right.

Watch this video below as I explain how a Light Transmission works and why we are clogged.
www.MyDivineDiamond.com

Write Down Your Realizations And Insights From Introduction & Starting The Practice

Affirmations

Positive Affirmations Uplift Consciousness

What actually are affirmations? They're just words. Everything is just words until it is connected to our true Higher Self. And through the practice of meditation, you're in a higher state of consciousness. There is a higher vibration being transmitted that is your very own Self. So, then affirmations, they're not to keep us in the world and attached to things, but this particular affirmation I find very, very good because, within it, it encompasses so much. And the affirmation is this:

I am whole, perfect, strong, powerful, wealthy, loving, harmonious, and happy.

And if you would like to add to make it even more powerful add:

Thank you, Divine, for my Magnificent, Beautiful Life.

See, the thing is, everyone is going to think thoughts anyway. The maya, the illusion, the collective unconsciousness of billions of people makes it very, very challenging for us to think true thoughts. So, what has been thought in the atmosphere is brought into our consciousness, into our subconscious. This is how it makes itself known to us as if it's our very own thought. And you know that this happens when a negative thought comes up. It's this resistance. It's this sleepiness in this lower vibration of consciousness, and it's very, very challenging to get out of it. We must use our willpower to focus. If we're going to focus on something, it's very, very good to focus on positivity. I'm not talking about your projects and your work, of course, focus on that. However, when these negative thoughts come up, replace them immediately.

I would recommend that for this month, use this affirmation until you know it off by heart, definitely. Say it as you're walking, even as you've just got the indicator on your car. Tick, tick, tick, *I am whole, perfect, strong, powerful, wealthy, loving, harmonious and happy. Thank you, Divine, for my Magnificent, Beautiful Life.* And just as you go to sleep, just to have that affirmation rolling around is very powerful. Now, you don't think of the affirmation when you're practicing meditation, but what you can do is just say the affirmation and then just do a lovely prayer to your own spirit and then just go into the Silence or the music, to silence the mind from all the other minds. That's why we listen to the music to begin our meditation and then for say the last 30 minutes go into stillness and silence. At the end of your meditation, just smile and repeat the affirmations again. Just say it because then you're in a higher vibration. The thought then of this beautiful affirmation is more powerful. *I am whole, perfect, strong, powerful, loving, wealthy, harmonious and happy. Thank you, Divine, for my Magnificent, Beautiful Life.* This world is created with thought. We create our world with thought. This world is created with thoughts.

Even Lord Buddha said *We are what we think. All that we are arises with our thoughts. With our thoughts, we make the world. Speak or act with an impure mind and trouble will follow you, as the wheel follows the ox that draws the cart. We are what we think. All that we are arises with our thoughts. With our thoughts we make the world.* You've heard this, maybe for some of you, that thoughts create our reality. Now, thoughts don't create our reality if there are all these other mixed thoughts going on. And we don't want to get caught up in thoughts creating our world, but because we do know that this happens, I think it's a very, very important point to realize that if you are going to think, it must always be positive. Positive thoughts hold a higher vibration.

I am whole. What does that mean? That means healthy. That means everything, doesn't it? *Perfect, strong, powerful, wealthy, loving, harmonious and happy*.

There was a man who was born with a lot of deformities. He was a little boy and a little bit crippled as well. I don't know how he found out about an affirmation, but this was over a hundred years ago. Perhaps his parents knew about positive thoughts. Maybe they practiced meditation. They told him, say this affirmation, *I am whole, perfect, strong and powerful, loving, harmonious and happy*. He used that as a mantra over and over again. And as he grew, everything became perfect and whole in him. He grew up to be a powerful man who helped the world with so many wonderful things that he did. Who is this man? This man was Charles Haanel, from the *Master Key System.* It's a real story. It's a true story.

This is a powerful affirmation. If you're going to think a thought, think a powerful affirmation. Of course, when we go into meditation, we do our best to not think because Eternity doesn't begin meditating you until you have stopped thought. That's when meditation happens. But when we are thinking it's important to remember to think happy thoughts and to say NEXT or STOP to any thoughts that are negative. They are not the Truth for you. They are an illusion. They're a lie attempting to keep you in a lower vibration. Write a gratitude list. You may know about this, but we don't do it because of this resistance of *I'll do something else* or because we get unfocused. We don't know how to concentrate our mind. Even if you're not doing it to become Enlightened, the practice of meditation helps you to focus your mind so that you become more empowered within yourself. And these negative thoughts don't have as much strength. Remember, there is only one power, God, but we have to be connected to that Spirit, this love, that is harmonious, that is happy, until we rise above even the harmony.

Please remember the subconscious mind and the conscious mind are what we are using for this particular body. But the subconscious mind is a computer. It doesn't know the past. It doesn't know the future. It only knows what it's told now. So, please remember this. It's extremely important. Now, some of you might say, *Oh, great affirmations, I'll do it.* And you'll do it for two or three days and then you'll forget. It is very, very powerful. Why don't you just do it just for this month? See what happens. Write it down. Look at it everywhere until it becomes part of you. Like when you're not thinking, you hear this beautiful mantra OM MANI PADME HUM. That means the jewel is in the lotus of my heart, Enlightenment is here and everywhere. Alternate both of them. *I am whole, perfect, strong, powerful, wealthy, loving, harmonious and happy.*

And don't look outside to see what's going to happen. Don't expect anything to happen and don't *not* expect anything to happen. Be non-attached. Just get into the feeling and the rhythm of this, especially when you're in a high vibration, after you've exercised, or while you're exercising and after you've practiced meditation because then you're in a higher vibration. So, then when you practice your meditation, it's going to be easier and easier and easier for you to melt into the Love, into the Divine Love.

This is why we use my Affirmation Power music. It helped me from a near-fatal car accident. And then because of those positive thoughts that were continually going through my mind, through the music, it brought me into a higher oscillation where I awakened to this Love of God. And then I went searching for God everywhere until finally, I realized that it was already within me. I met my Enlightened Teacher and then really got into the practice of meditation in ways that profoundly changed my mind, my life, my peace. God Bless My Teacher, Kundalini, Forever!!

If anyone could even have a moment of what this bliss is, this Kundalini, when it's awakened within you in every part of your body. I mean just focusing on the heart chakra, or the throat, or the third eye, or anywhere in your body, it's bliss. It's like bubbles of Light just purifying us. Using these affirmations, especially if this is new for you, is extremely powerful. And that's why my Affirmation Songs are so powerful because they go straight into the subconscious mind. The doubting mind does not have a chance to spit them out. And they work 300 times faster than just saying or writing them down. Although I do recommend you write them down and speak them. Use all the tools in your Divine Life-Changing Tool Box. As you're hearing the lyrics, *I am love. I am Divine. Love lives in me*. Letting these things go straight into the subconscious mind with the music is very powerful. The music and the lyrics of these affirmations go straight into the subconscious mind without your conscious mind playing with you and saying, *Oh, that's not the truth for you*.

This is what happened to me in the hospital. It happened because every time I said, *I am healed, I know I am. I love myself. I am my friend.* And the doctor was saying I probably won't walk again and if I do, I would have all these limitations, blah, blah, blah, blah, blah, all these steel plates all through my body, all these long operations. And when you're in physical pain, let me tell you, my friend, as some of you may know, and I hope some of you never know, it is very challenging to think positive thoughts. But I was willing to do anything. And so with the music affirmations, I sang,

I am healed, I know I am. I love myself. I am my friend. As the healing light of the universe surrounds me and flows through me, I know that **I am healed.**

Here is a link to my positive affirmation song
I Am Healed.
https://youtu.be/1ouKWAR7Roo

It is a positive lie you tell yourself so that it will end up being your truth. In one respect because my body wasn't healed you can think I was lying but I wasn't expecting anything. And I think that's why originally it worked so well because the melody, even just my own voice creating the melody, goes straight into the subconscious mind. But not only that, it actually gets you focused in the now, and once I had added the music, the vibration of the music itself, lifts you up and the lyrics become a new thought straight into the subconscious mind. And the conscious mind doesn't have a chance to reject them. And this also happens after you practice your meditation because you're in a higher **state of consciousness. And please remember, there is no such thing as a bad meditation. If you listen to three songs, just three tracks of** music, first thing in the morning, first thing, and feel, *As a* *sunbeam is one with the sun, I am one with God*. Take that into your meditation and *I am whole, perfect, strong, powerful, wealthy, loving, harmonious, and happy.* And then let go. Just let the waves of the music still your mind. What you're doing right now, deciding to read this, is against all that the maya would want you to do because it changes you. It gets you to that state where you want to do something positive, incorporating these powerful thoughts. And then going into the Silence, you're connected to all that.

There is the omnipotent, omniscient, omnipresent Light of Eternity, which is your true mind. Let yourself be happy with what you've got right now but know that there is more in that. Anything is possible. Everything is possible for you. There are no limitations in this dream world that we call life. I wish you an increase of life. And this is also what this does for you. It gives you an increase of life.

And what does an increase of life give you? It gives you energy, it gives you love, it gives you enthusiasm. And at the same time, peace and love. And I probably have said this, I don't know how many times, thousands, whenever your mind is attempting to judge another or they don't know what they're talking about or blah blah, it's your own self, not your Higher Self. It's this illusion attempting to keep you down because everyone is one. Let me just reiterate that. There are six and a half billion people on the planet *(At that time when Michele did this event. Now it is about 8 billion.)* and everyone has their own personality, their own culture, their own belief system, and their own way of thinking.

And then there is Eternal Consciousness which is Immortal. So, what is real never changes. And what is not real changes and fluctuates. What is real within you, within us, is this Light. Think of your spirit as the sunbeam that is connected to the creator, to the Divine, to Eternity. And that sunbeam is attempting to wake you up. *Hello, hello. I'm here. I'm one with omniscience. What do you want? What do you need for your happiness? I can help you go into the stillness, the Silence. Let me in.* Answer your Higher Self and say, YES, PLEASE.

We are one with this Spirit, this Holy Light, this omniscient, omnipotent, omnipresent, Divine consciousness. When we say, *Oh, I'm one with all people,* you're not one with their human attention. You don't want to be. So, don't think about other people. Do your best to go, *Next.* Don't think of other people. We don't want lines of attention on human attention. We are one with Eternity in them. It is the same ocean just coming through in different personalities, but not everyone is connected. In other words, of course, you're connected because you wouldn't be able to speak, or breathe, or move, or do anything if you weren't connected. Because once the spirit leaves the body, we know that we can't do much with that body. It just decays and it's gone.

There is this block of ice of human attention that needs to be melted away. Then you can hear it. It's a distant voice at first. You can hear it, the frequencies of Eternity. And then it gets louder and louder. Your hearing gets very, very acute. That's what I'm speaking about. You're not one with human attention. You are one with that Spirit. The activity of God is active in everyone. And that is the Truth for everyone. And knowing that Truth for you will assist you. I am knowing that Truth for you. You are one with that Spirit.

This evolution is fast however you must do the work. What is the work? Be positive, be positive. Stop those negative thoughts. You'll just create more and more worlds that you don't want. More and more situations that you don't want. Say it with me. *I am whole, perfect, strong, powerful, wealthy, loving, harmonious, and happy*. God in you is that, it is the Truth of who you really are. Just be happy and love. Just love, love Eternity. Not things, not people. Eternity in people. And then melt as one into The Holy Light. All you can see is this Holy Light. Everything else disappears. There is a hum throughout your entire being hummmmmmmm.

Write Down Your Realizations And Insights From Affirmations

How To Become A Conduit For The Light

Even A Small Light Removes Darkness

Freedom, freedom, freedom, FREED-OM. Today on this event I am going into something different within consciousness and it's going to be a much faster transmission for all of you. I am going to do everything I can to fill your hearts, your minds, and your consciousness with Light so that you will naturally be attracted to your meditation practice and that you will go for it for your Enlightenment.

Because you're here for freedom. Enlightenment is freedom. No more complaining, or hand-to-mouth this, or begrudging that, or *Why can't I get this?* Because when you have that type of freedom, everything that is required for success in life will come to life. Your mindset will advance and you will be very bright. Speaking about bright mindsets, God bless you, Olivia Newton-John. What a bright star. She will be forever in our consciousness. Beautiful lady. Are you ready, everyone, to experience this and to just to snap out of it? Just to snap out that maya where there are no limitations. Limitations are a lie pretending to be the truth.

Every single day I get requests to do a TV show, or to do a radio show, and I'm doing many every week. I did a magazine cover for Alexa for Amazon. I'm now one of the experts for that. I mean, it's nonstop. When I asked for no publicity, I didn't get any. And when I asked for publicity, it just came in, and the same can be true for you no matter what it is. Whatever you ask for when you're in this state of consciousness just flows in. We take action, of course, and market ourselves, however, when we do begin to take action that is when we have said to the Universe, *I AM ready*, and that is when many more ideas and opportunities manifest.

Are you ready? Everyone repeat after me.

I'm open and receptive to receive the beautiful, omnipotent, Holy Light.
I am open and receptive to give the Holy Light.
I am now a conduit for the Light.
So, everywhere I go, in thought, in feeling, and in my nature,
I know that this Light is nurturing everything,
And nurturing everyone,
Plant life, human compassion, healing, and beauty.
Because the Divine Presence always goes before me and prepares the way.
That is why I love my beautiful life.
I am open and receptive to becoming happier and happier and wealthier and wealthier.
I always remember as I leave my house or go anywhere to smile.
I am confident. I am strong. I am beautiful.
And I am so, so deeply thankful.
All that's left to say is my life rocks because of you, Divine.

Very good. Okay, so that's what I would like all of you to memorize. Just memorize it because these are words that have meaning that will absolutely vibrate to the highest level of frequency as you say them. This is a blessed prayer for you. You are all of that and so much more. And it's challenging sometimes to have Faith, Love and to be open and receptive and to truly surrender. You're surrendering by using these words. You're surrendering yourself to be a conduit. And that gives you that freedom. Everything is in Divine Right Order, Divine Right Action always.

Please remember your state of mind is the gateway to your success in your Enlightenment, in your meditation, in your finances, in your health and vitality, with the joy that you feel, with the Love that you can give, and with your compassion. It is a powerful thing, the mind. It has been given to us to be able to have that intention when the Light's coming through us. We have that intention, and we pray. Prayer is so wonderful. It uplifts your being. You feel great when you pray and say positive things about people. One of the things we are never, ever going to do is complain. Correct? Yes. No complaining. No blaming. Get out of jail for your mind. It will get you out of jail in any area that is diminished, and instead, you will be fully loaded with Light. And it is a discipline to give yourself happy thoughts when there are things going on in your life. It's not putting icing on an unbaked cake, I'm not saying to ignore the challenges, but to be brave enough to look at them and say, what can I do to change this? I know I can do something. Why am I going backwards instead of forwards?

Where's my enthusiasm for God? And meditation? Where has that gone? Well, let's not worry about the past anymore. Let's just brush the past aside. Are you ready? How are you feeling? Smile. Tell your face how you feel. I love what Yogananda said. *I am a bubble of laughter in the sea of Mirth itself.* Ah. Does that not say it all? Yes, it does. Thank you, Yogananda.

See your loved ones in your mind's eye happy, laughing, hugging and sharing good news.

Write Down Your Realizations And Insights From How To Become A Conduit For The Light

Meditating To Music

Music Makes the World Turn To The Positive

Today we're going to go back to basics for some of the people who meditated a while ago but have stopped meditation practice. Everyone has experienced some form of meditation. Anytime you're not thinking and you're gazing at a beautiful sunset, or if you're looking at your baby when it's just born and there's no thought, just love and unity, or when you're in deep sleep when there's no dream, when you pass a dream plane. Everyone has an experience of meditation where there is no thought.

The reason we are here is to become Awakened. And to become Awakened, we must silence our thoughts or do the practice that will eventually allow our thoughts to be silenced. I again thank our beautiful Teacher, Kundalini, because She taught me about music with meditation. Of course, always do your best to have at least 10 to 30 minutes of not much music. Bach, Mozart, and Beethoven have wonderful symphonies with which to meditate however Kundalini suggested other music that she had meditated on to assist her students by giving the music more Shakti Power. I could feel her Transmission as I meditated to the music. Then I just listened to the Silence after the music has stopped. At first, I did not think meditating to music would work for me because I had been meditating for many years with no music. However, when I first met Kundalini, because She was and is the real deal, I knew I had to have a beginner's mind. Even though I had been teaching all over the world, here at last was a True Enlightened Teacher who was willing to Teach me, so I got my ego out of the way and just basked in her Sunlight.

First of all, most of my music is purely to uplift you and to allow those pop affirmations from the songs to become new, positive thoughts. However, meditation music is different. The music (when you use a headset) assists in blocking out the rest of the world. And I always recommend big headphones, not those little things. Big headphones that cushion out the rest of the world so that at least you're feeling just your own thoughts and feelings, not the rest of the world pushing upon you. As you listen to the music, it actually helps bring Light to you as well. It's almost like having, well, it is like having a Light Transmission.

If you've never practiced meditation before, begin by doing 15 to 20 minutes every morning and every evening, lunchtime as well, if you can. It's wonderful to do it first thing in the morning. And so, if your routine is all regimented and you don't have any extra time, it's very, very simple. You get up earlier. Some people love meditation in the afternoons. There are certain times when people feel the Light more than others. I love it late at night when everyone else is asleep. That's my favourite time to just completely go away. It is so wonderful. It just depends on the person. Eventually, of course, you can meditate for hours because then the Light is meditating you. No matter what you do to start with, it tremendously helps stop the thoughts when you take deep breaths and make sure that your nostrils are clear.

Sit up straight. It's very, very good to get a space where you're just going to meditate and not do anything else in that space. Get a meditation mat. I got a brand-new, beautiful, round cushion the other day that's quite high and it's nice and firm and it's just lovely.

Begin by taking eight deep breaths, breathing in through the nose very, very deeply, and then very slowly out through the mouth. And meditation isn't for relaxation. That's visualization. You can visualize and get into a relaxed state. Even though, of course, later one of the benefits is you do feel more peaceful, which some people can call relaxation, however, meditation is a very focused experience. It's there for you to be very focused and assist you to shut out the rest of the world so that your Divine Presence can be felt. And even after just doing it for two weeks, if you're consistent, that is the key to be consistent, you will feel different. Your psychic abilities, your intuition in other words, will be clearer, there'll be less muck, you'll feel healthier, and you'll sleep better. You'll just be a lot clearer. It really makes a huge difference.

And even if there are lots and lots of thoughts that go on during your meditation practice, that's fine. People say, *Oh, I can hear more thoughts now than I ever felt before now I'm trying to practice meditation. I guess that's not working.* No, it's because you are not aware normally of all the thoughts taking you down every rabbit hole. Someone says banana and you start thinking of all the fruit you've ever had in your life. *When was the last time I had a banana? Oh, bananas have potassium*, and blah, blah, blah. And then you go down the thought rabbit hole. *Do I have enough potassium? Oh, hang on, am I late to get to the post office? Oh, what do I have to bring to the post office?* The mind goes down all these rabbit holes.

The main thing to begin with is don't try to stop your thoughts. You just do your best to stop the rabbit holes from going on. If a thought is taking you on a journey down a rabbit hole, say *NO, NEXT, STOP, I am here now.* Simply refocusing your attention will bring you back to stillness. Bring yourself back to your centre. *I Am here.* Focus on your breathing, your eight deep breaths. And then in the morning, it's very, very lovely to focus on your third eye, which is between your eyebrows and a little above. (When you do have a real experience, for me it came out of the middle of my brain.) But once it's actually activated, it's your whole forehead and nose, everything. It's all just hunka, hunka, burning love, that's for sure. Pulsating, burning love.

This will bring you clarity and focus. However, if you don't have to go to work that day, I just recommend heart chakra. And then in the evening, the heart chakra, which is actually along the Sushumna, along the spine.

Focus on the heart chakra being in the middle of your chest. It's not actually the heart, but it's along the Sushumna, the ethereal spine. It is exactly where you think it would be in conjunction to where the heart chakra is. It's in that spot along your spine. Because once that begins to become activated, you can feel a lot of pressure from all those tiny, little bubbles of Shakti, the bubbles of Light from the Divine.

It's activating, moving to help unclog the chakras to bring that Kundalini up so that the chakras can be activated. You don't meditate on your lower chakras. We meditate on the higher chakras to bring that Kundalini up and not just have it stuck there.

Let's keep it simple K.I.S.S Keep it simple and spiritual. Then you listen to three or four songs. And if you want to, you can use a mantra my Teacher gave me, which is now just part of my consciousness, which is so beautiful, OM MANI PADME HUM. Om, of course, is the infinite God. Mani means jewel. Padme, lotus.

Hum means heart. So, the jewel, the Divine, is in the lotus of my heart, literally. That's what it means.

And it also brings Light to your consciousness, and it brings Light to the world. And some people say, *Well, why don't I just do it in English?* Because it is a very ancient mantra that has been used in Tibet and Bhutan and many beautiful places since the beginning of the Buddha. You see these people doing the mantra all day and all night to bring Light to the world. It is also written all over their prayer flags. And they want the wind to go through the prayer flags because it is bringing that beautiful intention of Enlightenment to everyone in the world.

And if it wasn't for these beautiful monks and different Enlightened ones, this world would be a much darker place than it is. It's a very ancient mantra that holds power and it brings Light to you, but what is most important is it brings Light to other people as well. You are also assisting in bringing Light to other souls for them to Awaken.

And that is why we are here. Everyone thinks they're here for their own Enlightenment. We are here to help the Divine use us to bring Light and release suffering from the rest of the world. If your thoughts are rampant and are going down too many rabbit holes, gently say in your mind, OM MANI PADME HUM or Peace Be Still.

And the way I started doing it, probably because I'm a musician, I used to love to do it to Pachelbel's Canon. OM MANI PADME HUM. Or you could also do it when there's a back bass, or if there's particular meditation music that's rock and it's got bass. Where you can say OM MANI PADME HUM in time with a kick drum or the bass line, OM MANI PADME HUM. Just sing it in your mind not out loud. And then you are bringing Light to your consciousness and you're releasing the other thoughts. So, we're going to do that now and we're going to do it to Pachelbel's Canon.

Here are a few albums Kundalini recommended to me when I first started being her student. These are not my albums, but I'm recommending them to you as well as I have meditated on them a lot and I love them.

You can purchase these albums on iTunes or Amazon, however, the fourth album we have included a link for you to download the album for free.

Mystic Spirit Voices
by Lesiëm

Odyssey of Love
by Kaanchman Babbar

Sacred Memories
by Cybertribe

Samurai
by Zazen
To download this album for free just go to:
https://ramatalks.com/meditation-music/zazen/samurai/

Write Down Your Realizations And Insights From Meditating To Music

Spiritual Anatomy

Our Entire Body Is A Spiritual Being

Also see the video on Kriya Yoga

First of all, let's talk about Kundalini and a Kundalini Awakening. The Kundalini is the energy that is at the base of the spine that everybody is born with. Every single person on this planet is born with this blood of the Life Force of the Divine that takes you into different dimensions that helps activate chakras. And that's a lot of work to activate the chakras depending on what you've done in past lives. However, when you follow these instructions and you're having Light transmitted to you as well, it is tremendously powerful. When I first received Light from Amma and Mother Meera, before I met my Teacher, it felt beautiful. However, when you meet your real Teacher it is so much stronger. I knew from the moment I saw Her that I would do whatever it took to be her student. And I know you all agree it was the best thing that could happen to ALL of us. Because of Her we are here today.

We have the Kundalini, or often called Shakti. I call Shakti the energy that is coming from the Eternal coming through my consciousness and being sent to you. This Shakti helps awaken your Kundalini. This Shakti that's sent to you, that's transmitted, it's Light. It's a fast, oscillating vibration of golden bubbles of the Divine, which is in a different dimension than this one. It is brought through someone who has Awakened, or from someone in early Enlightenment, or from someone who has been transmitted with the power to be able to transmit Light.

So, we have this beautiful Kundalini, it flows through the Sushumna, the beautiful ethereal tube that runs from right at the very base of your spine. Well actually it's more like in between your bum hole and your genitals. I told you, highly technical. Now why do they call me such a spiritual person? And so it's sitting there and it wants to come up. That's its purpose. It isn't wanting to just sit there dormant. Like legs want to walk, like hands want to express themselves, eyes want to see, ears want to hear.

And that beautiful Sushumna is in a different dimension, but it's still on your subtle body. Your subtle body is your true body, and the Kundalini is sitting there. And once it starts flowing up this ethereal tube, which is blocked, you can just look at it as being blocked with lines of attention and cobwebs and grit and sludge and all these different experiences that have kept it blocked.

And what happens is, that Kundalini is in a Divine Dimension, and it begins to flow up into the Sushumna. It is the blood, the Life Force of the Divine. And it is tiny, little, smaller than atoms, bubbles of light that are oscillating. And just like when you see atoms when you've looked through a microscope and you see that they bump up against each other, so does this energy. They're just oscillating, vibrating at non-human speeds. And it is vibration, it's a vibration of Light. And that vibration starts scrubbing and cleaning the Sushumna to allow it to become cleared so that as it flows up, it can activate the chakras.

Some people say, *Oh, my chakra was like asleep and it needed to like you know like wake up.* No, once the chakra is activated, it's activated forever. It's activated in this particular lifetime. It's a Divine Dimension. It's like a wheel, a doorway to a Divine Dimension, where gifts are given to you that every person has the ability to receive. Because everyone has the ability to be able to see into the future, or to be able to feel and know where someone's coming from. If someone's going to do the wrong thing by you or if someone's going to do the right thing by you, immediately with no judgment, you feel love. You see glowing Light everywhere. Buildings disappear. You have strength and powers, but you're not doing it for those powers. They just naturally come. You get to experience flying through the Stargate into different Divine Dimensions and universes, different world planes, Buddha lands, and amazing, indescribable experiences through the third eye as well. And I always recommend focusing on the heart chakra and the third eye. They're both important. However, why is it that for some people, it's just really, really challenging for them to even start feeling their chakra?

When you start feeling the heart chakra become activated, you feel these bubbles of light, it almost feels like a ball at the back of your spine. You can actually feel it putting pressure there, because it's a tremendously high oscillation of tiny vibrations of Light. They're not quite gold. It's not like a gold that you'd find in this particular world plane, but it's vibrating God. It's scrubbing you clean and you can feel it like a pressure, however it is not painful. And when it starts, when you are getting Light, when people first become part of the Mystical Experience or first start really becoming cleared and getting the Light transmitted to them, they feel it, because that Light ends up hitting their brain. All that Shakti is in the brain to help stimulate that part, so that the Kundalini can flow up to reach its Beloved, the crown chakra.

One of the reasons why people find it hard to have that Kundalini flow into the Sushumna, actually begin to flow, is because they haven't yet conquered the ability to balance the Ida and the Pingala nerves. This is extremely important, and those that have been with me for a while, I have taught you Kriya Yoga breathing. I wasn't taught that with my Teacher. However, she sent so much Light, that whatever I needed to know just seemed to come to me from past life experiences or from a book I read somewhere. I started doing the Kriya Yoga breathing because it is so important that both nostrils are clear. For most people, when they're breathing, one nostril is closed, and the other one is breathing. And so Kriya Yoga breathing eventually assists you to have both of your nostrils clear 90% of the time. Sometimes there might be something in the air. So, you might get a little sneeze and one of the nostrils may be blocked. That's when we use organic, saline nasal spray, harmless. You just get it, it's organic, it's only got saline in the spray. And it actually really, helps people that have had certain sinus challenges or allergies as well. It's very good.

The Ida and the Pingala actually stop at the top of the spine. So, that's why when that becomes clear, people will feel that their third eye is sort of moving in and out. You have to actually see it as well. You can feel it, though, when it first starts to be activated and you can start breathing through that third eye, literally breathing through that third eye. And some people will feel their third eye in their sinuses, literally half of their forehead, right down in their nostrils. They'll feel a little pressure and maybe a little pain as well as those sinuses become clear. It is extremely important that the Ida and the Pingala are in harmony. And the way to do that is through Kriya Yoga breathing, making sure that both nostrils are clear.
The more you do the Kriya Yoga breathing, the more you are practicing the balance for the Ida and the

Pingala. And this will cause that Kundalini to flow into the Sushumna at last and come up.

The Ida and the Pingala, these are the two energies that flow along the spine. Ida is a nerve, it's extremely sensitive, and it flows along the left side. And the Pingala flows along the right side. The Sushumna of course flows directly upwards and downwards. I mean the Sushumna is there, but the energy, once the Sushumna is clean, flows up and down between the Ida and the Pingala and eventually is activating and coursing through those chakras until after it comes up and down enough times those chakras become activated.

We have many different areas of the nervous system, but the nerve centre in the area of the third eye, or the Ājñā chakra, the space between your eyebrows, is extremely sensitive. That's why it's important that they are both working in harmony. And when I send the Light, I'm assisting with this so that you don't get into trouble or into problems.

So, the Ida flows along, I'm going to repeat things a lot, the left side of the spine and it comes around and it converges onto the left side, as it comes up and down, and then the Pingala flows along the right side of the spine, circles around and converges on the right side.

And then, of course, after that there's the crown chakra, the thousand-petal lotus as they say. But boy, when it's on fire, it's on fire.

There is the convergence of the Ida and the Pingala at the third eye, which is actually right in the middle of your brain. My Teacher used to call it like a swan, but you feel it through your third eye. And what I found once I started, my subtle consciousness started going through my body. I was in the brain and I could see it, and I could see this blue flame, like this blue line of light, coming straight from the middle of my brain through that part of my forehead, and then bam. Then you go through the Stargate. Some people say to imagine the Light is outside of yourself coming into you, but it was actually the other way around in my experience.

So, once that blue light comes through, that is the magical, Divine key that opens the Stargate. And with the Stargate, you first start experiencing a flash of Light. You're meditating and there's no thought, and all of a sudden a flash of Light with a loud, fast sound. So, that's the beginning of the Stargate. And I experienced many, many, many flashes of Light before I actually went through the Stargate. And I didn't know that that's what it was. I thought, whoa, just a flash of Light. Yay. It was only later that I recalled being a small child and flying into space.

I find some people say to just focus on the heart chakra at night. But what I used to do is the heart chakra, and then I would do the third eye if I knew that I had a few hours to go for it. And then you are just going to gently focus after you've listened to the music, after you've meditated with the music, to help stimulate even more Light.

Then you just listen in the Silence and you just calmly listen to your breath and eventually your breath actually stops. And when your breath stops, oxygen is still flowing through your body. You are looked after. And what could happen sometimes is people are like, *Oh my God, I stopped breathing,* and then their meditation has gone out the window. They have to start again. And that happened to me a lot back in the day. But eventually you realize you're safe, and that everything is working to still that mind.

You just keep all of those external things out of your mind and that's why it really helps with the music and the headphones. And I used to listen in the Silence with the headphones still on. Eventually I would take them off, but it really assisted me to feel stillness. But it's just up to you. It depends on how quiet your neighbourhood is, just gently placing that attention between the eyebrows and making sure that the energies are flowing evenly between both nostrils. What I would like you to do, even if you don't know about Kriya Yoga breathing, is just do your best right now to get a tissue and blow your nose. And all you're going to do is listen to the music. Focus your attention, listen to the music, sit up as straight as you can. Don't put your head up, don't put it down, just straight ahead. If you feel it going up or down, just do your best to bring it back so that the spine can stay straight. But if the spine can't stay straight, it's still going to work. Trust me, it's still fine. You just have that intention that it's straight if you can't physically make it straight and you're just going to focus very, very gently on your third eye.

You can put a little bit of oil there between your eyebrows and above, or you can scratch it a little bit if you need to. But those who know how to go deeper and see that blue light coming from the middle of your brain, do that. But eventually, if your mind has become still, you don't have to focus there anymore. Surrender, let go, and let the beautiful Light assist you to clean out that Sushumna.

But by putting attention to the lesser flowing nostril right now, and every time that happens, it will gradually open. Eventually, they will both flow freely.

Just be aware and patient because Awakening will come. It requires consistency. Doing it every day. And eventually, you will have a very good ability to focus your attention on anything that you are doing for your work. You'll be able to see more clearly, your inner seeing, you'll know things. You'll just know, those Satori's will come more and more frequently, which is really beautiful. Now we're going to bring our attention to this right now. Are you ready?

Write Down Your Realizations And Insights From Spiritual Anatomy

Third Eye Chakra Meditation

Ājñā Chakra
A New, Magical Divine Dimension Is Reached
Through The Third Eye

Today's topic is all about the third eye. Oh my goodness. I'm really, really happy. Did everyone bring their sandalwood powder, and rosewater, and candles? Anyone? Or a face mask?

Because you put it on wet between the eyebrows and a little above and then it dries. And you can feel it as it dries, tightening the skin. That's the idea to put it on your third eye. The sandalwood is such an ancient, beautiful fragrance and it has some beautiful, ancient, mystical qualities that can really assist you.

Third eye, third eye. Now you guys have heard me speak about when I first went through the Stargate, right? I'm happy to speak to you guys about anything. The third eye is situated in the pineal gland. I did not know this when I first saw that flash of Light in the middle of my brain. The ancient name for it is Ājñā Chakra.

Okay, I'll tell you again. When it first happened, the first time, I actually saw this shooting, lightning-blue electricity come from the middle of my brain. Because when you go inside of your body, you can bear witness, 360 degrees, when you're in certain states of consciousness, and you can also be inside your body. I've been inside my brain and my body so many times, it's absolutely fascinating. And it's not me choosing to, it's my Higher Self putting me somewhere so that I will understand. I saw it shoot through and I would always see this little dot of Light and sometimes, after meditating for a long time, I'd get a flash. A flash, and it'd be like an explosion. And I didn't know that was the beginning of the Stargate.

The first time I went through the Stargate, I'd been meditating on my third eye, scratching it, doing my sandalwood, really focused. And I shot through the Stargate and that was my first experience. And it's like if you've seen the movie Stargate, it's very, very similar except the noise, the rush, the buzzing is more intense. It's over the top. And then if you're blessed enough, which I have been many, many times, you go right through it until you're in a different dimension.

Now, when people leave the body, temporarily, they don't go all the way through the Stargate. Usually, they will be met halfway into another plane of existence until they are brought back into their body. This has been documented many times in those who have died where the doctor has brought them back to life. Your consciousness can go all the way through a Stargate to a different dimension, and then through another Stargate to a different dimension. Until you keep going, and then you come back into your body when you realize, *Holy shit*, the minute you have a thought or think this is amazing, you're back into your body so fast. It's like whoa. Some people have had those experiences and they absolutely freak out and go to the doctors. I was like, *Again! Again! Take me again.*

And so that is the third eye, that's that little dot that you'll see that you focus on. And then different parts of your brain light up and you get to know things. I left school when I was 15, however, that does not mean that I am uneducated. My education has been through real experience and yes, many mystical books, and travelling all over this beautiful world always seeking God.

When there's something that has been downloaded to my consciousness, I still don't understand sometimes what it is that I'm saying. But at the same time I do. It's like all of a sudden someone's speaking Japanese and you can understand it perfectly, even if you don't know how to speak Japanese. It's like that. You may still not understand the Japanese language, but you know what they're saying. It's the only way I can explain it.

The reason that the third eye has been spoken about for years, especially once they knew about it scientifically, is because of its relation to the pineal gland. The pineal gland is what brings the light and the darkness. It is used for you to see light, colour and shade. And I remember having a really deep meditation where I had this nectar come down my throat and it was the most incredible, euphoric taste and feeling. Scientists are studying all of this and they're also looking at the Mystical side of it at last.

Now do you want to try the third eye meditation? Yes. Enough teasing.

Rosewater really does clean your aura so beautifully. And if you mix sandalwood powder in the rosewater you will feel and smell an ancient vibration. Once the third eye is completely activated, all the sinuses light up because there are tiny sensors and nerves that are all part of the third eye. And so put the sandalwood paste all around that area.

And what happens as it dries, you can feel it contracting, which absolutely 100% assists you so beautifully to just focus there because otherwise, whoa, there's a rabbit hole, there's another rabbit hole. And just listen to the music, always doing your four deep breaths. At least making sure both nostrils are clear and if you need to, because you're finding your thoughts are going rampaging somewhere else, you just gently bring yourself back. Take a deep breath, feel it again, keep your eyes closed, and then just focus again. And we're going to do that now to three tracks. Here we go. Do your four deep breaths. If you do want to light a candle for a minute, that helps with the third eye as well. Keep the candle flame level with your eyes without having to hold it up.

What I want everyone to do today is really, really focus on your third eye.

Scratch your forehead in between so you can really feel it. And I want you to visualize, to start, a blue light coming from the middle, like a laser light. Like sapphire glowing, coming from the middle of your brain, straight out through your third eye. Let's see if we can get some flashes happening with you guys today. Are you ready, everybody? Let's do our four deep breaths in through the nose, and out through the mouth. If you have to blow your nose, do it. But we really want to be so focused today, and if you can't keep focused on your third eye, I want you to sit up as straight as you can, and just listen with both ears as if both ears are in balance so that everything is focused on being totally centred.

Practicing third eye meditation brings the Kundalini up eventually to the crown chakra. You probably won't get rushes of Kundalini for a while, however, one day that door will open. Third-eye meditation will activate that Divine Portal. And I know it's challenging when you just want to go to your heart chakra because it feels so yummy, however, I'd always do my heart chakra at night and my third eye every morning and it worked for me. Everyone do that as well. We want to invite that Shakti up the Sushumna until you have your flashes of Light, more and more flashes of Light.

Here we begin with our four deep breaths. Making sure, of course, that both nostrils are clear. I'm going to be sending a lot of energy to your brains, to your crown chakras while we're doing this. So, really focus, take advantage. Here we go.

Write Down Your Realizations And Insights From Third Eye Chakra Meditation

Heart Chakra Meditation

Anahata Chakra
The Heart Chakra Is A Doorway
To Eternal Bliss

Or what I choose to call the yummy chakra.

I love this particular album that Kundalini gave us years ago to meditate on. She meditated on it for hours. And then the last couple of months before my Enlightenment, my full Enlightenment, I'd been through the Stargate a lot and had all these out-of-this-world experiences happen. However, when I was really gone, I was listening to a couple of different albums and then I would go into the Silence for a couple of hours afterwards. This album I LOVED and still do is called *Blocking The Sky* by *Approaching Nirvana*. Oh, how Mystical. And you wouldn't think it's a meditation album, but it is because it really works your heart chakra and it's so important to really feel the bass and the drums and feel like that's hitting your heart chakra.

The heart chakra is along the back of your Sushumna, the ethereal spine, but you'll feel it right through your entire body, 360 degrees around there. You can focus in the middle of your chest, but if your heart chakra has already begun to become activated and you're feeling the pressure in your spine, you can just focus there as if it's a beautiful, round, golden gate waiting to open. More like ready to activate and explode and take you to another Divine Dimension.

As we listen to the first part of the song, we're all going to be conductors for an orchestra. We're going to get into a nice vibe. And then after that, we're just going to be still and completely focused on those drums. After this, we will go into silence with no music and we will simply listen with our eyes closed to the Silence and feel the Stillness. For example, say you've just meditated to quite a few songs. You still have your nice noise-cancelling headset on, and you just listen to the Silence. You are listening to, with both ears, sort of coming from the middle of your brain out, whichever noise you can focus on. If you're just hearing the high-pitched noise, it's not tinnitus. It is the beginning of the sound of the Oms. There are so many different harmonies in these Oms. So, just listen and be still and take a deep breath and open your eyes. Now we're going to go through a few different methods that will assist you.

The thing I love about the conducting is you get an opportunity to really listen to the music. Okay, there are violins coming in here. Oh, the piano's coming in again, and you listen. It's listening to music and then when you close your eyes, you really hear the music which assists us greatly in stopping thought!

Write Down Your Realizations And Insights From Heart Chakra Meditation

Pathways To Enlightenment

Are You A Bhakti, Jnani, Yogi, or all three?
All Paths Lead To God
Some Simply Take A Little Longer

Now today, because of the fact that we have some new members, and also because of the Light transmission people, I thought we'd go into some basic meditation practice. It will also allow you to determine whether you are a Jnana Yogi, Bhakti Yogi, or Yoga Yogi.

A Bhakti is a lover of God. You see God in everything and everyone. And it doesn't mean that there's duality. A Bhakti Yogi usually finds they are quite sensitive to the world when they're young, but they also want to see everybody happy. They have this love, and they're not sure what it is. Sometimes they seek it in people, places and things but nothing satisfies them. They are soul-sick, and they are on a search.

They usually are people that love animals and nature. And sometimes they could go through depressions in their life before they find that thing that they're looking for. They're not sure what it is. And they're like, *Oh my God, I have all this love to give, can't someone feel it?* But it doesn't mean that if you are not a Bhakti that you won't become a Bhakti. Can anyone relate to that?

And then there's Jnana, Wisdom Yoga. Except, people do not truly understand what Jnana Yoga, Wisdom Yoga is. It is what Ramana Maharshi Bhagavan was all about, he called it Jnani, even though he was a Bhakti, as well. Because those who are fully at that stage, oh my goodness, well, they're everything, all-encompassing, because it's all within them.

That Wisdom Yoga, Jnana Yoga is, *Who Am I?* The Japanese Zen Teachings and the koans were all about Jnana Yoga, giving impossible questions like, *What's the sound of one hand clapping?* and all these other ridiculous things that someone's trying to figure out. And eventually, they get to a point where they say, *Oh, there is no answer. The answer is in the Silence. Silence is the answer.* That's where the Wisdom is, that is where God is. When all questions that could possibly be asked have been answered, and it's *Soham. I Am That. Who am I? Who am? Who? I am. I Am That. Soham. (Pronounced So Hum.)*

Some people think that Jnana yoga is finding out what they're afraid of. But that is not Jnana Yoga, not true Jnana Yoga. Some people take it too literally when they hear a teacher speak about what they're afraid of. Finding out where the fear comes from is a very good thing to do. It's an exercise in releasing yourself from fear.

This is more mindfulness, being aware of where the feeling is coming from, than Jnana Yoga. So, you find out, *What am I afraid of losing that I've already got? What am I afraid of not getting that I want?* Maybe you're not afraid. Maybe it's the person sitting next to you who's afraid of something and you're picking up on their fears. It's recognizing what you're afraid of so that the fear will be released. And then you are free. Then whatever it was you were afraid of not getting, you get, because you're not worried about it anymore. You don't have fear, and you don't have a need of *want, want, want.* This is a good exercise, as long as it doesn't take you down the rabbit hole of question after question after question. Because the mind has infinite multitudes of rabbit holes that you could go down, that will take you down a lot of different topics or experiences you have in your subconscious mind. This is where people have to be careful when they're going too deeply into it, when the way to release fear, of course, is the Light. The Light melts away those fears, the more it is transmitted to you, the more you practice your meditation, the more your attachments to the illusion dissolve. That's the true way to release fear. But if there's something happening right in that moment, and you want to release the fear, when you can recognize what the fear is then it will dissolve.

Sometimes it's not even a fear. Sometimes, when you are practicing your meditation and all this Light is coming to you, it can start activating your heart chakra. And the subconscious mind doesn't know what it is. It's like, *Oh, what is that feeling?* And so, it'll go down the rabbit hole of all you have thus far experienced that is all in your subconscious filing cabinet. It will usually connect with anxiety and make one feel *Oh, I'm anxious, or there's something wrong with my heart,* when it is not. It is just that the activation of that heart chakra is so different from what you're used to. Eventually, you will feel like your heart is out of your ribs. When that heart chakra, that Divine Dimension, is activated fully, the fears are gone. And you can see what is and what isn't and have very strong intuition about people and things without any judgment. It's a very beautiful experience to simply bear witness with no judgement.

And then there is Yoga. And Yoga is, of course, the practice of meditation, and mindfulness. There are a lot of different practices in what is called Yoga. A Yogi practices meditation, they don't just do Jnana Yoga, or Bhakti, even though they can do all of the above. With our teachings, we don't just teach one method.

It's important to be educated in all so that you can utilize all of the methods to assist you when you're going through the world, which can get very tricky to manoeuvre sometimes.

I am going to read to you from something that Swami Muktananda wrote about his Teacher, his Guru Nityananda. I love this because it is very true. *A person's feelings are influenced by those around him. Then these feelings create thoughts, and thoughts produce a state of mind. And the state of mind gives rise to questions. So, a person asks questions, according to his feelings.* Now doesn't that make sense, isn't that simple? And people don't realize that they think that their feelings come first. But your feelings are just influenced by people around you, and vibrations around you. And if you've been a person who has not been able to quiet their mind during their lifetime, when you first start meditation practice, you become sensitive to vibrations around you and other people's feelings, much more so than before when you were blocked.

That's why when someone first starts meditation practice, I've often heard them say, *Michele, I have more thoughts now than I ever did.* And that's not true. This is a very good sign, it simply means that now you are aware of all those crazy thoughts, and now you learn how to quiet them down during meditation. This is good. The first thing is awareness of these thoughts, so that we can quiet these thoughts down, and eventually they do. You'll just hear the ringing of truth, those bells, those whistles, the Oms, the vibration of the bees, whatever beautiful sounds that Eternity makes, and you'll have access to those Divine Dimensions, where it's beyond sight or sound from or of the world.

You can be influenced by those around you. Eventually, of course, it doesn't influence you, you just see and feel where someone's coming from. If someone gets in a lower vibration, and they don't realize it themselves, you can gently snap them out of that lower energy. If they're open to this, great. If not, walk away from them if they're influencing you to also go down in oscillation. There is no judgement. You will know by how you feel if this is influencing you in a negative way. If you know a way to bring them peace and happiness without being influenced by their vibration then all I can say is WONDERFUL you are gaining power. Actually the highest way you can bring them peace and happiness is to be happy and peaceful yourself, and then your vibrations will influence them. And that is very cool indeed.

The mind starts thinking thoughts associated with what the vibrations are around it if you are not as yet a strong enough swimmer who can navigate the tides of human emotion. And then those thoughts, whether they're positive or negative, high thoughts or low thoughts, produce that state of mind. And then, that state of mind will give rise to all different sorts of questions according to the person's feelings at that time. And it really does make a difference to the way that person is going to live.

[Continuation of the reading from Swami Muktananda] *The people who follow the path of Devotion, Bhakti Yoga, would come to Bhagavan Nityananda and say, "Oh, sir, are you a Bhakta?" "Yes", he would say, since everyone who is coming to him would have all these different states of mind. And followers of Ashtanga Yoga would ask him, "Babaji, are you a Yogi?" "Yes", he would answer, then Vedanta, those who pursue the path of Knowledge Wisdom, Jnani, would ask, "Swamiji, are you a Jnani, a knower of the truth?" "Yes", he would reply. And with that, they would all argue with each other afterwards. The first said, "I asked him, he said he was a Bhakta". The second, "I asked him too, and he's a great Yogi", and the third, "No, he's a knower of Truth. He's a Jnani".*

In this way, they would debate and argue with each other from their own point of view. The fact is that Bhagavan Nityananda was all of these. He was a Bhakti, a Yogi, a Jnani. He contained everything. But who can really understand this, how can there be Yoga, union with the Divine without Devotion? How could there be pure knowledge without Yoga? How could one realize the Divine essence without having attained pure knowledge? How could one attain pure knowledge and lasting bliss without God realization? Are supreme bliss and Nityananda different? In reality, it is impossible to separate Devotion, union with God, and knowledge. Bhakti means Love. And Love is only another name for joy. Joy arises when the restlessness of the mind is still. Creating a still mind is called Yoga. Through Yoga, knowledge, Divine Wisdom arises.

The idea of Yoga makes people uneasy. They think yoga means turning your back on the world, living in a mountain cave and eating wild roots and berries. Not so. Every soul in this world practices Yoga, to some extent. A person follows certain rules of conduct, regularity, getting up, eating, getting to work, going to bed, exercising. Whatever kind of work one does requires some degree of concentration, Dhyana. Painting for instance becomes beautiful through the artist's concentration. In the same way everyone has some experience of Love, Devotion, Bhakti, and knowledge, Jnani. Everyone feels devoted to someone or something through discrimination. One distinguishes between good and bad. So, Devotion, Yoga, and knowledge are all essential and interwoven parts of life. So, that is why Sri Gurudev would answer, Yes to all those questions.

Beautifully written. I highly recommend you read Swami Muktananda's book *Play Of Consciousness.* **It is one of my favourite books.** After reading the first chapter I felt waves of Shakti immediately, and I knew the Teacher (though he had left the body) had gifted us all with a very powerful Transmission of Truth through his Autobiography.

Write Down Your Realizations And Insights From Pathways To Enlightenment

Which Spiritual Aspirant Are You?

Always Aspire To Do More, Have More, Be More

I am going to start this Teaching Session by reading a little bit from the Yoga Aphorisms of Patanjali's *How To Know God*, translated by Swami Prabhavananda, who was a disciple of Swami Vivekananda, a Mahasiddha and one of the main disciples of Sri Ramakrishna.

This reading is from aphorism number 45 in the second section. And the aphorisms are from Patanjali, teachings of a great Enlightened Vajra Buddha.

As the result of devotion to God, one achieves Samadhi. [Samadhi is when you have melted into the ocean, when Eternity, the Universe, whatever you choose to call God, Eternity sweeps you up into pure consciousness, bliss, timelessness. Pure Love. It's not a practice anymore.] *This is what is called Bhakti Yoga. We have already mentioned these Yogas or paths to union with God. Now for the sake of clarity, it will be well to define the ones which are most important. Bhakti yoga is the path of loving devotion to God. It can be expressed by means of ritual worship, prayer, or japa* [and japa simply means the action of speaking your mantra, pronounced jarpa by the way]. *It is the cultivation of a direct, intense, personal relationship between worshiper and worshiped.*

[Continuation of the reading] *In the practice of Bhakti Yoga, some special aspect of God or some Divine Incarnation is chosen so that the devotee's love may become more easily concentrated. For those who are naturally drawn to this approach, it is probably the simplest of all. And there is no doubt that the great majority of believers, in all the world's major religions, are fundamentally Bhakti Yogis.*

So, Bhakti is when you just feel a love for God. It doesn't have to be, by the way, a particular saint or deity. It can simply be within you. A Heart Glow of Divine Love. You just feel a great devotion and love for the Divine. And when you have great love and devotion for the Divine, it does make things a little easier. However, not everybody naturally has this. So, let's continue to the next way. Certain people have certain inclinations, so it's good to hear about these as well.

[Continuation of the reading] Karma Yoga is the path of selfless, God-dedicated action. By dedicating the fruits of one's work to God, and by working always with right means toward right ends (to the best of one's knowledge and ability at any particular moment), one may gradually achieve wisdom and non-attachment. Action is transcended through action with non-attachment. The bonds of attachment fall away. The wheel of karma ceases to revolve. Peace comes to the spirit. And Brahman is known. Karma Yoga is the path best suited to vigorous temperaments which feel the call to duty and service in the world of human affairs. It leads such people through the dangers of overeagerness and undue anxiety and shows them how to find the inaction that is within action, the calm in the midst of the turmoil. Sri Krishna's advice to Arjuna in The Bhagavad Gita is largely concerned with the practice of Karma Yoga.

So, if you're the sort of person who doesn't naturally feel a great love for God, however, you do feel good within yourself when you are of service, whether it be of service to a Teacher, or service to the homeless, or to other people, then Karma Yoga may suit you. St. Teresa of Calcutta was a Karma Yogi and a Bhakti because she loved Jesus so much, it caused her to take action and treat every single person as if that was Jesus that she was treating. So, she was a combination of Bhakti and Karma Yoga, taking that action. I love the way it's explained here because when somebody has that sort of vigorous temperament and you go and do things for others, and you are of service, that is just as important and it can lead that person to Enlightenment because they just know that that's what they're here for, to be of service. And they feel so much better when they do that. And it's a really beautiful path. It's a magnificent, giving path.

Next one is Jnana Yoga, which is wisdom yoga.

[Continuation of the reading] Jnana yoga is the path of intellectual discrimination, the way of finding Brahman through analysis of the real nature of phenomena. The Jnana yogi rejects all that is transient and apparent and superficial, saying, "not this, not this", and so comes at length to Brahman by the process of elimination. This is a difficult path, calling for tremendous powers of will and clarity of mind. It is not for ordinary people. But it has attracted and made saints of many remarkable men and women who would otherwise not have embraced religion in any form.

And I actually know a gentleman, it took him years and years, but he actually did Jnana Yoga and it was so challenging for him, but he did it. It just happened naturally. He didn't have a Teacher. This was years ago. And he said to me, it was just a process of elimination. It was just within him to do that, to just ignore anything he saw in front of him. Not this, not this. That's not real. It's an illusion. It's an illusion. And he had not read *A Course in Miracles*. And *A Course in Miracles* is based on Jnana Yoga. *A Course in Miracles* is all about, no, this isn't real, this isn't real. That's not real. But it does take years to do it. He didn't have a Teacher transmitting Light, but he did become Enlightened, but with absolutely no attachment to anything ever again. So, he found it difficult to really feel anything in this world and it was just a little challenging for him to realize that that's the way he got there. And he's now on the path of Bhakti Yoga to bring his feelings and love for the Divine into his being. Then he'll go into true Blissful, Loving, Compassionate Enlightenment.

You may naturally have these qualities and feel that you are attracted to a particular path, however I teach and use everything so that you can find what appeals to you the best. At a time when you are not sure of something, then you use wisdom yoga, you go to the core of it. Who am I? What is this all about? You go to the core of it until there's nothing there. Zen is very much Jnana yoga. What's the sound of one hand clapping? Is there really a sound when a tree falls in the forest if you're not there? Zen koans are meant to get the student, the monk, to get to the point where the answer to the question is not answerable until the students get to the point where there is nothing in their mind. This practice is a form of Jnana Yoga.

[Continuation of the reading] Raja Yoga is often called the yoga of meditation. It is not so easy to define as the other Yogas, since, in a sense, it combines all of them. For meditation may include God-dedicated action (i.e., ritual worship), discrimination and concentration upon a chosen aspect of God. Raja Yoga is also concerned with the study of the body as a vehicle of spiritual energy. It describes, for example,

the nature and function of the various psychic centres, such as the lotus of the heart, already referred to (chapter I, aphorism 36). Since Raja Yoga stresses the value of formal, scientific meditation, it is primarily for those who desire to lead monastic, or at least predominantly contemplative lives. But it should certainly be studied by every spiritually minded person. It teaches us the importance of technique in prayer.

Everybody's different and everybody has a combination of all of them at times on the path. At times you may want to use Jnana Yoga so you can get to the root of what is causing some stress in your life. And, of course, meditation is extremely important, but Raja Yoga is more of a contemplative meditation. It's like going into a question, Who Am I? Or just contemplating a flower, or getting to the root of it. Yogi Bear was a yogi. *That's right, Boo-Boo. I'm smarter than the average bear.*

I was just naturally born a Bhakti from past life experience of devotion. But I also have used Karma Yoga and Raja Yoga. And as I said, you can use all of them, and you will find that you are predominantly one more than the other. And if you find you can feel that you are one more than the other, you still use your meditation, you still do your best to love the Divine. But if you find that you're more of one than another for example, if you enjoy being of service to others, you've got to do it with non-attachment and without feeling the need for someone to say, *Oh, good for you, you're such a good person.* That sort of selfless action, as long as it's not being a victim, is helping others because you know that someone needs to do it. Not to get a pat on the back.

Something else I wanted to read to you is from Patanjali Yoga Sutras Commentary by Swami Vivekananda and he talks about liberation. Once the Atman, the Light, God within you shines forth in its own pristine nature as pure consciousness, well then, you're done. You're Enlightened. I love the way he says it. *Nature's task is now done. This unselfish task which our sweet nurse, nature, had imposed upon herself. She gently took the self-forgetting soul by the hand as it were, and showed him/her all the experiences in the universe, all manifestations, bringing him/her higher and higher through various bodies till lost glory came back. And he/she remembers his/her own nature, God nature, Divine Self. Then the kind mother went back the same way She came for others who have also lost their way in the trackless desert of life. And thus is She working without beginning and without end. And thus through pleasure and pain, through good and evil, the infinite river of souls is flowing into the ocean of perfection of self-realization.*

That is so high, that is so beautiful. Nature is God, the source of everything. Mother Nature is there helping us. We are made from Mother Nature. Mother Nature is not the maya at all. The maya is the collective consciousness of everybody's thoughts. It's thoughts, that's it. We stop our thoughts. We take action that is kind and loving. We stop ourselves when we're complaining. We make sure that we're grateful for this life. We absolutely kick ourselves in the arse when we're feeling sorry for ourselves. And we take action, we do something. We do something to change our state of mind because you can change your state of mind very, very easily. You just switch your attention. So, did that make some of you think, *Oh, what am I? What am I?* Did you think about that? Could you feel what you were predominantly?

Write Down Your Realizations And Insights From Which Spiritual Aspirant Are You?

Bhakti Yoga

Fall In Love With The Divine

Today we're going to speak about stillness combined with Love. I would love for you to really get this today because when you can feel stillness and it's combined with Love, you go into very high states of consciousness. Or you go not into something, you go away from something, away from the world. Sort of silly pedanticism with verbiage, isn't it, when you're talking about Mysticism and effects of the unknown.

First of all, before we go into a stillness meditation, let's talk about judgement. Because for your mind to become still and free of thoughts, and your body as well, it's very, very important that you become extremely aware or mindful of when you are judging others. For example, if somebody lies to you, does this affect you?

See, this is the thing, we cannot take anything personally that comes, whether it's a lie or a truth, from other people, because that shows that you don't yet have that stillness within. The things that trigger you, be very aware of them. Who cares if someone lies to you, none of it is real. It's the same as if someone is saying something truthful. It doesn't make any difference. I mean, some family members, the rubbish they say, I don't care. It makes no difference to me what they say or what they don't say. Especially if someone's lying. What if they're lying about you? Does that trigger anyone? If you know someone said something about you that's not true? Okay. There is more nodding.

We can't let that bother us either. If we can really, really get away from the ego being touched by anything, who cares if someone's lied about you. When people complain about you or lie about you, or lie to you, what they're doing is they're covering up their own fears. They'd rather have it deflected onto something or someone else than face their own shadows and their own fears.

Does this make sense? I've repeated it many, many times, but still, *Oh, I'm so upset that that person said this about me,* who cares? Who cares? We cannot take it personally ever, ever, ever. Because it's not personal. It's about them.

You cannot take anything that happens in this world personally, even when it feels personal. And this will ingrain in you more stillness. How great is that?

You're looked after by the Divine no matter what. So, it's fine, it's all good, all of it, all of your life is good.

The prayer of St. Francis of Assisi is exquisite.

Lord, make me an instrument of your peace
where there is hatred, let me sow love
where there is injury, pardon
where there is doubt, faith
where there is despair, hope
where there is darkness, light
where there is sadness, joy

O divine Master,
grant that I may not so much seek to be consoled as to console
to be understood as to understand
to be loved as to love
for it is in giving that we receive
it is in pardoning that we are pardoned
and it is in dying that we are born to eternal life

You say this magnificent prayer and then just feel the stillness. Feel what you just felt from that prayer. If we can live in this way, we will never be worried about what anybody says about us ever again. You'll never say, *Oh, they don't understand me.* Who gives a shit? Let you be understanding to them. *Oh, they don't love me.* Love them. It is just perfect. The two most perfect prayers I've ever heard in my life are this one, and one from Thomas Troward, *May there be more of God in me than me.* So, then you're never afraid of what anyone says ever again. Sticks and stones, etc.

And to remind ourselves to create this stillness, we must Love, we must feel that Love. And for me, it is thinking of my Higher Self as the Divine Mother, because she gives to me everything that needs to be known. And she allows me to be a complete conduit for all of you.

And when we're praying for others, stillness comes into our heart because we feel Love. When you begin to feel compassion, there's more of God in you than you, because God is all compassion, all Love, no judgment at all. You can bear witness and see that a person may be acting like a total arsehole, a prat, but there's no judgment. Sounds like there is, doesn't there? But there's not. You're just witnessing it. You're not reactionary to it. And then you don't even notice after a while if people are being nice or nasty. I mean, I have had a couple of conversations with students where they were really disrespectful and rude to me, but I didn't feel it within me. I just felt that they're going through some fears and I'll just have to do whatever I can to let them rise up. And if they need to vent onto me to feel better, I will allow that.

I will allow that because of the fact that they don't mean to be doing it, they don't realize what they're doing. And usually, they do realize later and they apologize. *I can't believe I said those things to you, Michele.* And I tell them, *I never took it personally.*

You just needed to vent. And I was fine with that. It's all good. It doesn't happen very often, but it does happen sometimes because there's just that Love there. I just see the Divine in each of you and it's exquisite. And that's what I want you to see in everybody as well. Not the person, not the personality, but the Divine Presence. When you are going to speak to someone that is tricky, because some humans are tricky, I want you to say, *My Divine Presence is connecting with their Divine Presence.*

Say to yourself*, We have one Divine Presence, and that's what's communicating today, not what's coming out of their mouth. And I will shut up. I will do my best not to interrupt, not to feel reactionary. I will do my best to just be still. I'm going to find the stillness within me before I speak to this person.* And you'll find that the people that were usually a little tricky will be really lovely to you in that moment. All of a sudden, maybe the next moment they'll be horrible to the next person they meet, but to you, it will be almost like this wall of Light that they can't penetrate. They can't feed off your energy because they can't get to it even if they're trying. So, when they can't feed off your energy, they usually stop trying to because you're not allowing it anymore. Is this making sense to everybody? Heads are nodding so yes, it is making perfect sense.

You're just not allowing it anymore. Because it's not real. This is how we find stillness combined with Love, by being mindful and being very, very aware. Especially when you have said something to someone, and they've taken it the wrong way, and then you feel within yourself, it's like an itch, that you've got to explain yourself. *They've got to understand what I meant by that.* Who cares? They've forgotten. They have forgotten.

When you feel that itch gnawing at your ego, just quieten it down. It may be screaming to be let out of the shoot you have in your mind, ready to cause havoc. However, YOU CAN control it. Just say, *STOP*, breathe, and let it go. It's not real. It doesn't matter. They don't need to understand you. Maybe they did understand you and you just misunderstood them understanding you. And even if you did get misunderstood, understand, don't take a stand. Understand that it doesn't matter what other people think. It doesn't matter. It's none of your business. They're probably just thinking about themselves anyway. And then you just sort of live in a Love fest.

Write Down Your Realizations And Insights From Bhakti Yoga

Kriya Yoga

Always Remember To Breathe

Also see Spiritual Anatomy

Clearing Nostrils

With Kriya Yoga Breathing, first of all, we have to make sure that both nostrils are clear so that we can breathe in deeply through both nostrils evenly. We've got to make sure that both nostrils are clear. By doing this, you hold the right nostril with your right thumb, and then you breathe out four times from your left nostril, you breathe out. That's where you might need the tissue if you've got gunk in there. And then you breathe in through the same nostril four times. And then you hold the left nostril with your left thumb and you breathe out through that right nostril four times, keeping your left thumb on your left nostril, and you breathe in through the right nostril four times. Now you keep doing that until both nostrils are perfectly clear.

That's the beginning of Kriya Yoga, to make sure that both nostrils are clear, so that the Ida and the Pingala nerves along the spine and the Sushumna, along the ethereal spine, and the actual physical spine, will be in harmony.

Because people have gotten in lots of trouble, especially those who've meditated and had a Kundalini rush, but not a full awakening, and they feel like they're going to go a little insane because they've been meditating just on their crown chakra and they haven't had the Ida and the Pingala balanced. Now some people say to visualize, as you're breathing in and out, the Light coming up through the spine and then going down through the spine. And I don't really teach that anymore because I found that had my mind thinking too much. However, I did do it for a few months until I just felt it more empowering to simply do the Kriya Yoga breathing as it allowed me to truly surrender while meditating.

The main thing for me was to be able to breathe through both nostrils, and I would do deep breathing sometimes for 20 minutes, and then I'd start my meditation because my mind would then be still. And as I was meditating, if the thoughts came up again, I would make sure both nostrils were clear. And even if it was just eight or ten breaths, I would do the deep breathing until I felt stillness enter my being.

Spinal Breathing

Visualizing the energy did assist me for a few months, as I mentioned, so now I will share with you how to do this visualization of the spinal energies. Please begin blowing that nose and making sure both nostrils are clear. Now stay with your eyes closed. We're going to go straight into another practice. I'm going to do some spinal breathing, which is still Kriya Yoga.

It is a simple method of moving your attention between the base of the spine and the crown of the head. You are coordinating the flow of energy with your physical breath, the physical body, and the mind. This is really Kundalini Yoga and Kriya Yoga, they go hand in hand. And Kundalini Yoga is, of course, chakra meditation. But these are very, very important to remember because we want to clear up that Sushumna.

The root chakra, it's literally located between the genitals and your backside (posterior), and it's the opening, it's the mouth, or the opening to the

Sushumna channel. So, what I'd like everyone to do, we're going to do this as well, you're going to combine this. You're going to breathe in and tighten your posterior and visualize, doesn't matter what colour, I don't care, just the feeling, just the intention of Light coming up through the Sushumna. Because we don't want the Kundalini to flow along the Ida or the Pingala. You want it to flow into the Sushumna directly and evenly.

So, we focus while it's flowing up through there, tighten it up, see it flow up. Then feel your intention on the crown chakra, as its flowing through the top of your head and then sort of visualize Light coming back down through the top of your head, down right through the centre, beautiful, golden Light flowing.

Now, focus on your third eye, and if you're breathing, just breathe gently into the nose and very softly and gently, slowly out through the mouth. Just focus on your third eye and just listen to the Silence.

Write Down Your Realizations And Insights From Kriya Yoga

Silent Meditation

*Gertrud von Le Fort said
Silence Is The Language Of Eternity*

People sometimes teach in very complicated ways, but there are certain people who will get it in a complicated way. They require to learn something and find it dramatic and passionate. Everyone has a different personality, a different way of understanding Truth. For some people, it's more scientific, you don't have to love God. You don't have to be a Bhakti to become Enlightened. But boy, after you're Enlightened, then you will. Everyone's got a different way of understanding Enlightenment. But the bottom line is it's just to stop thought. And so when I really, really, really got that, that's when I started doing silent meditation. Not any thought, not *Who Am I*, none of that. I was doing the **Soham** a lot, *I Am That*. And then one day I realized I am not anything, well not of this world. I'm not anything. I've just got to shut the f... up. I must still my mind completely to be free!

I would practice meditation with the music until I really felt my mind becoming still. And then I would just sit there with my spine straight and I would listen. Which is what I would do until there was no thought. And if thought came up, I would bring myself back to the centre of my brain with both ears open and focus on silence. The way that I kept having Stargate experiences was by stopping thought and all the other practices to assist me to stop thought. Kindnesses to others, not being selfish, tithing to people, all of those things assist because eventually when you do stop thought, it's God's grace that pulls you through the Door. Grace. No matter what you do, you honour the path, because it comes from your heart, that's what you're supposed to do.

With this meditation, I want you to do everything you can to stop thought. And the best way to do that is just to listen to the music. Sit up as straight as you can. Don't focus on any chakra this time, just keep both of your ears open. And what happens when both of your ears are open, you can sort of feel that your third eye or your crown chakra will start to buzz and tingle, and you'll feel that heat. Because just listening with both ears is very, very powerful. Whenever a thought comes up, just be gentle with yourself. Just go back to peace.

I loved what someone told me last week. He said he meditated for two and a half hours the other night and it was just terrible. Couldn't get his mind to quieten. And I was so happy because he meditated for two and a half hours. Because when you do it and it's really a challenge in that particular moment to stop your thought, it's doing a lot. The fact that he went for it is all that matters. As our beautiful Kundalini used to always say, *There is no such thing as a bad meditation. All effort is rewarded.* If you do a lot of exercise before you sit down, then your body relaxes, but it's also oscillating at a higher vibration. So, that does help stop thought. Exercising first is a powerful tool.

There are lots of different tricks you can use to stop thought, but the fact that you make the effort, because I don't know how many times I'd be sitting there, and thoughts would come back up. You're doing everything you can to stop those thoughts. But every effort makes a difference. Listening to the Silence and this particular track I am about to play is really great.

Say for example, you have your favourite playlist, you get all that Light transmitted to you through the music, and then you put that track on at the end. And then afterwards just sit there as long as you can in Silence. And it's actually good to have headphones kept on as that assists silence tremendously. You can lay down afterwards if you would like. However lay flat on your back with no pillow and continue to listen with both ears.

Write Down Your Realizations And Insights From Silent Meditation

The Stargate

Travel To Divine Dimensions

Also see Third Eye Chakra Meditation

There are many, many ways to stop your thought. Someone was saying to me that they started having a flash. They were meditating, and then they laid down and were about to go to sleep. And then they had that flash, and that flash, which is very loud, wakes you up. That is the beginning of the Stargate. Because the Stargate is a tunnel to a different dimension and when you experience it the noise is literally out of this world. They attempt in the movie *Stargate* to have great sound effects however it is indescribable. Saying that, let me attempt to describe the sound. Like buzzing and roaring, but not at all disturbing. It's like a million buzzing bees taking off in a rocket ship. This high, high frequency that takes you into different dimensions.

I said to her, what is happening is you've been meditating, but then you've gotten sleepy, and just as you're about to go to sleep, thought has stopped. And so you have a flash of Light because thought has stopped. So, if you want to meditate for quite a long time with music sitting up, and then lie down flat on your back, thought will stop.

This happened to me because my back was getting sore years and years ago. So, I laid down on my back without a pillow and I'm still meditating. And I sort of went into a bit of a trance I guess, and thought had stopped. But I was sort of in between sleep and trance and my first flash came. So, lying down, you can still experience that.
Every moment that you have stopped thought, a flash will come if thought is completely stopped, and there

are no flying clouds of thought either. Even Krishna said to focus, and just notice that there are clouds floating by, but don't take any notice of them. You don't want any clouds of thoughts. That's the whole thing. Shankara taught it perfectly. And it's been said that if you can stop thought for eight minutes, you'll go straight into Enlightenment. That's why it's so important to remember how to stop thought with every flash you have. And then it's like, *Oh, I didn't realize I just had a whole meditation with no thought. Whoa, here we go through the Stargate.*

But if you have the thought that you weren't thinking, well, then you're back in your body again. So, that doesn't work. But stopping thought is so important. It is vital, and consistency is also important. Even if you only did 15 minutes a day of meditation, which is ridiculous if you really want to go into high states like those, because once you start having those high experiences and meeting beautiful beings and going to different dimensions, you would say to yourself, *Oh my God, I can't believe that I spent so much of my life not meditating to now have this experience. I have wasted precious time on nonsense.* It's mindfulness as well. Mindfulness is to have no thought. As I said, when somebody says, *The lights are on, but nobody's home,* you say, *Thank you very much. I've been meditating.* That used to be a blonde joke once upon time. Oh, the blondes in the audience are laughing.

Write Down Your Realizations And Insights From The Stargate

Mala Beads

108 Is The Magic Number

Also see Meditating to Music

Someone was asking me about prayer beads and how to use them. See, when we use our mantra, OM MANI PADME HUM, that means the jewel is in the lotus of my heart. Om God, Mani Jewel, Padme Lotus, Hum Heart. It also means Enlightenment is within me, Enlightenment is everywhere. This is why all of the monks in China, in Bhutan, in Tibet, in India, do the OM MANI PADME HUM mantra over and over again because it brings Light to your mind AND to the world.

What you do is you sit up straight, as you normally would when you're about to do your meditation practice. You want the beads that are 108 beads. You do your deep breathing. First of all, you can have the music going if you want to, and you're just going to do your OM MANI PADME HUM mantra. You can do it out loud or you can just do it in your mind, which is preferable. You do not have to say it fast, do the mantra at any pace you feel assists with stopping other thoughts.

You can take a big deep breath if you want to, but you do your OM MANI PADME HUM mantra until you get to the top bead and you've done it 108 times. This practice is very beneficial to your meditation practice. If you find that when you begin your meditation practice one day, your mind is just going everywhere, you just get your beads, OM MANI PADME HUM, OM MANI PADME HUM, OM MANI PADME HUM, in your mind until you get to the end. And then you'll find that your mind has quietened, which is the whole point, to stop thought. It's beautiful because it's helping you quieten your mind and you're bringing Enlightenment into your consciousness, you're bringing that beautiful mantra also to the world.

Meditation is of course so many things, but the main thing is, keep it simple, stopping thought. KISS Keep It Simple and Spiritual. There are many, many different practices I experimented with over the years to assist in stopping thought.

Our beautiful Teacher, Kundalini, taught her students really beautiful ancient methods, such as the OM MANI PADME HUM mantra, and then I would add it to the music. You listen to a song. You can really OM MANI PADME HUM along to just about any music really, just in your mind. Drums that are four on the floor are great for OM MANI PADME HUM. Rock and roll, three-quarter time, not so good for OM MANI PADME HUM. That's why anything with Pachelbel's Canon is good. You can go, OM MANI PADME HUM to four on the floor. Even if it's just a string instrument, you can just sort of let the OM MANI PADME HUM float.

You've got to give space for the thought to stop. So, if you're using your mala beads, you just go, OM MANI PADME HUM, that is there to bring Light into your consciousness but also to replace thoughts with the mantra. The mantra OM MANI PADME HUM, brings Light to your consciousness and it also brings Light to the planet. And then stop and don't start again until the thoughts have started again. Then you do your OM MANI PADME HUM. See, so many people don't understand, and then it sort of annoys them. It's sort of like, OM MANI PADME HUM OM MANI PADME HUM OM MANI PADME HUM. And you're not giving yourself that space to have a still mind, which is what it's all about. Does that make sense to everybody? Of course, it does. You're intelligent, beautiful people.

I will say it again let's keep it simple. Kiss, kiss, kiss. Keep it simple and spiritual. What is meditation practice? What is the goal? To stop thought. Just stop thought, because once your thought has stopped, you are in Divine Union because God doesn't live in our heads, not in the consciousness of the maya. It's beyond that, beyond the doubting mind, beyond the world. And you can also have a different perspective of this, by thinking of the world as Enlightenment. Everything is God. So, if you can just change your perception of the world, okay, it looks like it's out here, but you are actually omnipresent in this world. You are every leaf on every tree that I can see out there right now, and the Divine that created you, created that tree, you are the oceans, you are the sand, the lakes, the water you are one with everything.

That's why every day when I have a shower, I bow to that water. I thank it for blessing me and healing me. It's all part of us. We're all one. And so, when you can look at the world as God, as Divine, as the Eternal, everything's been created by the Eternal. You look up at the stars, it's all you. We were made from the stars. Everything that's fallen to this planet we are part of, we were created from this. There's nothing, nothing on this plane, that is an inanimate object. Everything is vibrating.

Therefore, when you go to practice your meditation, you are already in Eternity. You're already in the Eternal. You are just there to quieten your mind, which will give you Union. It's very, very simple. And use all of the different tools that you've been given to assist to quiet your mind.

Yesterday I was talking about mala beads and how people don't use them correctly. You've got to just touch one bead, roll it around in your fingers, and say the mantra OM MANI PADME HUM. Because OM MANI PADME HUM for the mala beads is just to assist you stop your thought. But how are you going to stop your thought if you're going OM MANI PADME HUM really fast? There's no feeling, just a whole lot of noise in your head.

So, that's another excellent way. Just OM MANI PADME HUM Everyone do that with me now and then you'll see. You'll see how long you can stop your thought for. It's very fascinating, everyone. OM…….MANI…….PADME……HUM…...

I could stay like that in the breathless state for many yummy moments in the timelessness. Just one OM MANI PADME HUM. Don't you want to have that experience too?

All you have to do is do your best to quieten your mind after you've listened to the meditation music. Keep your headset on, and if thoughts come back in just OM MANI PADME HUM in silence, no music, nothing. Keep doing that until you start getting flashes of Light very regularly. Everyone attempts to make it too complicated and it is simple.

All of this practice and consistency eventually has us really experiencing being a lover of the Divine, a True Bhakti. You don't have to feel a lot of emotion when you're meditating. You want to just be still sitting with your spine straight. If you do feel a lot of emotion, any kind of emotion, even frustration, PLEASE do not give up. Simply begin some Kriya Yoga deep breathing and you will feel calm again and peace will grace you with Divine Love. Eventually, what happens is you start getting that heart glow. You start feeling the tingles regularly. After meditations like that, you'll just walk outside and you'll start experiencing Divine waves of ecstasy coming through you and you'll begin to really be able to feel when I'm meditating for you, when I'm transmitting Light to you. That will become stronger the clearer you become.

If you really do not have time here is a beautiful Divine Quickie to assist you to have a beautiful day. Take a deep breath. And repeat, *The Divine Presence is with me. And the Divine Presence has gone before me and prepared the way. This moment is magical. Every moment of this day and night is magical.* And then just be quiet. It takes less than 60 seconds. How does that feel? Amazing, right? You do that just once an hour, 60 seconds, 59 minutes, give one minute every hour to your Higher Consciousness, to your Divine Higher Self, and your life will be heaven. Doing that once an hour is powerful. Because, eventually, you will find yourself doing meditation consistently every day because you'll be in that vibration and you'll feel it. And whenever you are still, that Light will come in and start meditating you.

Write Down Your Realizations And Insights From Mala Beads

Gazing Meditation

Gaze Into The Divine And Be Forever Changed

One of the things that I first found absolutely amazing was gazing. I wasn't gazing because I was told to gaze a picture, I just was so in love with Babaji and this particular painting of his that I just would gaze it until there'd be no thought after a while, gazing softly into those beautiful eyes.

And then the painting of Babaji started winking at me, and he started blowing me kisses after a few months of gazing his picture with love, it came to life. And I gazed Babaji a lot because it assisted me to stop thought so easily to the point where I was not blinking or even noticeably breathing. Thoughts were completely stopped and I'd close my eyes again. And if it was a daytime meditation or morning meditation, I would then, if I found thoughts were coming back, I would gaze the beautiful photo of Paramahamsa Yogananda *[Autobiography of a Yogi A MUST read]* because he was just above Babaji on my wall. So, then I would start gazing Yogananda and he would start morphing into all of these different beings. And then I'd notice when their pictures would disappear. I was in meditation. Thought had stopped!

Write Down Your Realizations And Insights From Gazing Meditation

Bells And Singing Bowls
Bells Open The Door To Eternity

I started using a bell that I would ring over my crown Chakra in a clockwise circle and I found it to be a beautiful experience. I would listen until there was no sound left and I would experience true stillness. I would practice my Kriya Yoga breathing. After my Kriya Yoga breathing, I would wait a while in the Silence before I began my meditation with the music. I would get myself really still with my spine straight. Then I would get the bell. And I now sometimes do this over your photographs. When you listen to the bell until it's completely stopped ringing, it brings stillness. I also do this with singing bowls which you can make sing or you can hit gently on the side to hear a unique and beautiful ringing.

Kundalini used to say that when you hear bells, be still and listen because they open a doorway to the Divine. I know this is true because now I can FEEL such beauty when I hear bells. No wonder everyone loves jingle bells at Christmas. They make everyone feel uplifted and happy.

Write Down Your Realizations And Insights From Bells And Singing Bowls

Candles

Candle Light Attracts Angels and High Beings

When we have the intention of using candlelight for prayer or meditation, it brings in such beauty. Angels are soaring, I mean it's just incredible. So called dark energies don't like candlelight, particularly when you're doing it as a way to bring in the Divine Presence into your heart and Consciousness. To assist you, think of that candle flame as a representation of the Divine Light. You look at the candlelight as if is your own inner Light, which is a beautiful thought. What we do is bow to our candlelight because we are bowing to our own inner Light.

You're going to gaze the candle and then you're going to give thanks. Next, you are going to do a prayer internally in your mind. In other words, don't talk, and just give thanks for as many things as you want to express your appreciation more fully. Now gaze the candle for a little bit longer or for as long as you are feeling the stillness and love. When you can't gaze it any longer, you will find you naturally close your eyes. As you do, focus on your heart chakra and let go. Make sure you're sitting up straight. You may also do this for another person. Gaze the candlelight as if it is their own Light you are gazing and do a prayer of thanks for them. Here is an example. *Thank you beautiful Divine, Holy Light. This candle represents ….. and I give thanks that everything that brings her/him happiness is now in their experience and that every day, in every Divine Right way, they are Richer and Richer in Health, Good Fortune, Happiness, and Peace of Mind. Harmony Reigns Supreme in her/his life.* What a beautiful experience to pray for others in this way, quietly, without mentioning it to anyone. It is just between you and your Divine. YUMMY!

Write Down Your Realizations And Insights From Candles

Mudras

There Is Power In Our Hands

You're going to learn a lot about energy and the different intentions for the different mudras. As you'll see when you're looking at my Golden Statue of the Divine Mother and Protector of The Buddhas, Mother Tara, that She is doing some beautiful mudras. And if you look at a lot of different Buddha statues, you can see the different mudras. And now we're going to learn about the mudras and what they mean because energy comes from our hands, our feet, our eyes. It's incredible. It's miraculous. And when we go back into the ancient times, they're not just doing mudras as a nice little Indian dance. They're doing them because it's power. It's incredible.

If you look at Padmasambhava or any of the different deities, and look at Sri Ramakrishna, you will see their mudras. Sri Ramakrishna allowed only two photographs taken of him and he is doing two different mudras. He's doing the Apana mudra, and you'll learn about that mudra in a minute. When he's in deep Samadhi, he is naturally doing a mudra. He was not taught about mudras, they just came to Him from the Divine when he was in deep Samadhi. It is great to actually understand what they mean now because you can practice these mudras to assist Divine Energy to flow. Just when you begin to experience early Enlightenment, there are different things that you begin to understand as the Holy Light uses you as a conduit for healing, uplifting, and Enlightening. Clearing the way for all good to flow forth into your experience and for those you love. And Sri Ramakrishna was sending Light to his disciples when those photographs were taken. It's incredible that he allowed just two photographs that we can still to this day enjoy and gaze.

As we grow in consciousness, as we practice the mudras, they start to come to us naturally. And as we move our hands in certain positions, we begin to actually experience and witness Light shooting out from our hands. You can be out at dinner and start doing mudras under the dining room table and make the whole restaurant filled with gold happiness and harmony. Once you've Awakened, you can see the Light flow forth and it's really a great blessing, it is Divine, Beautiful Grace. Let us begin with the question, what is a mudra?

Well, a mudra is a Sanskrit word, which simply means sign. A lot of people, if they've taken yoga classes as in exercise yoga, can probably use quite a few mudras, especially if you've done hatha yoga. Or as I said before, if you look at any image of any of the Buddhas including Tara, there are so many different beautiful statues of different Buddhas and they've all got a mudra going on.

Something's going on there. And that's for a reason because every mudra has a very, very powerful meaning and Divine Intention. When you see it in a statue, that's the likeness of an Enlightened being that was sending Light to the world through all the little meridians in their hands, in their chakras.

And mudras really do have a much deeper, spiritual significance than some people realize. If you've ever seen a video of the Thai and Balinese women dancing, they're beautiful ancient dancers, you'll see that it's in their DNA that their fingers can bend backwards and they can do these amazing mudras. So, there's a lot going on there. Let's begin with the first mudra.

Gyan Mudra

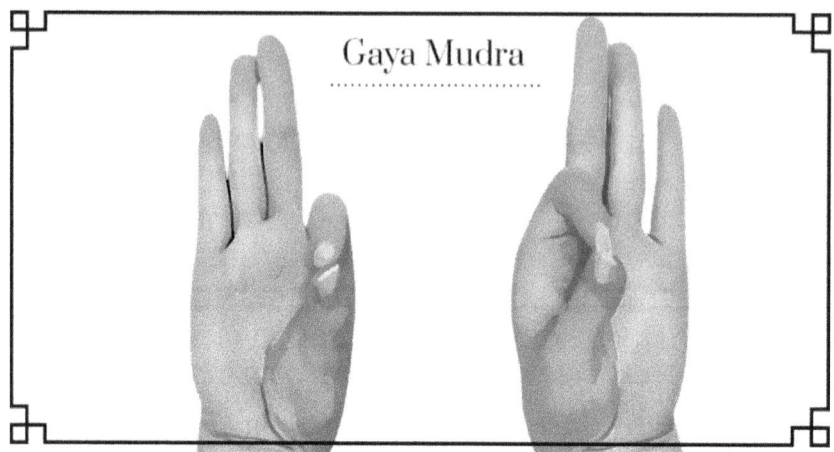

The first mudra is the **Gyan Mudra**. The Gyan mudra is the mudra of knowledge, and it's something that you may find yourself doing naturally when you're speaking with people, when you're communicating, using your hands. What you do is touch the tip of the thumb to the tip of the index finger with the other three fingers stretched out as much as you can, stretch them out. And as I said, it's the mudra of knowledge. It enhances Divine Wisdom. The tip of the thumb has centres of different glands that really, really start activating different meridians, which really does help your meditation practice greatly. And there's no particular time duration for any mudra. You can practice by sitting, standing, lying on a bed, whenever you've got the time to do them. You'll find people when they're teaching, you'll see them doing this unconsciously, doing the Gyan Mudra, because it increases memory power, it sharpens the brain. And what I love about it the most is it enhances your concentration, which of course, is what it's all about, Alfie. It's about Enlightenment, it's about meditation, it's about stopping thought. And so, you can do this particular mudra with your hand out straight or with your hand up as you can see our hand model beautifully doing.

Vayu Mudra

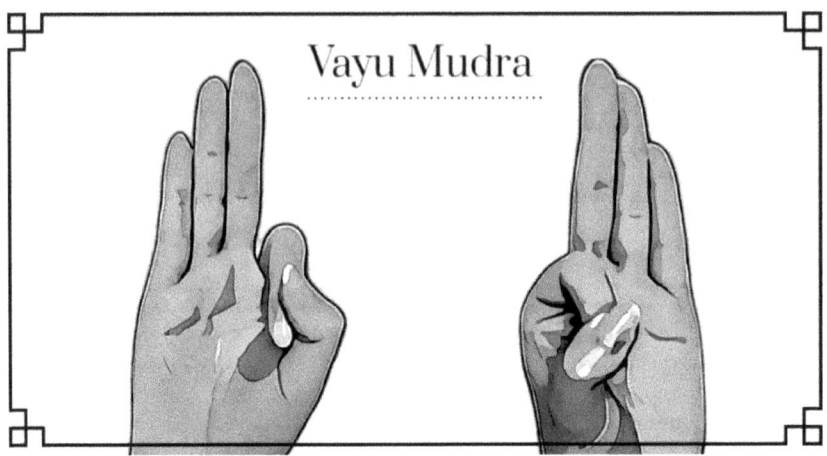

Great. Now let's go onto the second mudra. The **Vayu Mudra**, the mudra of air. You keep the index finger on the base of the thumb and press with the thumb, keeping the other three fingers straight as you can, as we did with the Gyan mudra. This absolutely assists you to enhance your concentration, your meditation practice, and it also enhances your immune system, which is a great benefit. And the practice of this mudra you might want to do a little longer because it really is quite powerful to assist with arthritis, and a lot of different autoimmune diseases. And it also, again, is great to practice doing this either with the hands out or straight up. So, that is a beautiful mudra. The mudra of air, the VAYU, the Vayu Mudra.

Varuna Mudra

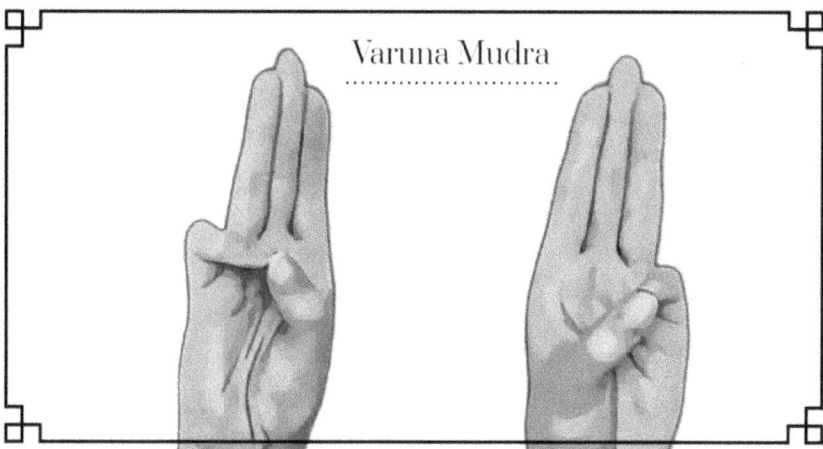

Now the third mudra, oh, who likes water? Who loves water? We are made of water. This is the **Varuna Mudra**, the mudra of water. It's a very simple mudra. It doesn't take too much practice. It's really easy. You just touch the tip of your little finger to the tip of the thumb, and the other three fingers are stretched out. It's so important to reiterate yet again, stretch those fingers out that aren't holding a mudra whenever you're doing these, as straight as you can. It balances the water content within your body and it also blesses the water in your body. And if you use this mudra when you are blessing water, when you say to the water, *I love you so much, you're so beautiful,* and you do this mudra at the same time, it actually blesses the water even greater. It's just a really powerful but very simple mudra to be able to activate that beautiful blessing of water within your body.

Dhyana Mudra

Now here we have my favourite meditation mudra. This is interesting. A long time before I was Awakened, when I would meditate, I would do the **Dhyana Mudra**. And you will see that this is really the Buddha's Mudra and it is one of the greatest Dharma Buddha Enlightened Mudras. You will see practically every Buddha statue holding the Dhyana Mudra triangle. I love to do this. It happens to me naturally. I like to keep the thumbs right up as you can see our beautiful hand model is doing, and you just have that sitting in your lap while you practice your meditation. A lot of people think that they're supposed to do the Gyan Mudra when they're doing meditation and you sit there with the Gyan Mudra on your thighs, but it's sort of a little challenging to do that if you want to meditate for hours.

So, the Dhyana mudra, the triangle mudra, it balances you, it balances your body, it keeps your back straight while you are doing the meditation. So, this is my favourite mudra for meditation practice, and it is the meditation mudra.

Linga Mudra

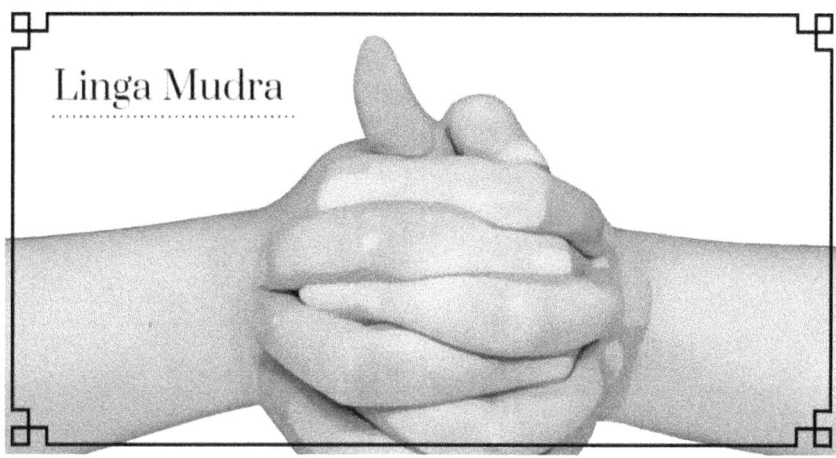

Now this next mudra is a little bit different. This one is the **Linga Mudra**. It's the mudra of energy. It's the mudra of Kundalini energy and it will activate some of that powerful Kundalini heat. As you're practicing your meditation, you interlock the fingers of both hands and you keep the thumb of the left hand vertically straight and encircle it with the thumb and the index finger of the right hand, as you'll see our beautiful hand model doing, and it generates that Kundalini heat in your body. It's absolutely so wonderful and you will receive so many health benefits from performing this mudra.

As I said, it does produce a lot of heat, but if you really want to go for it with your Kundalini Awakening, well then this is a good one to do. But I wouldn't do it for longer than say five minutes. You don't want your hands to sort of lock up, but it's a great one. And that's number five, The Linga Mudra of Divine Energy.

Suchi Mudra

Now, this next mudra looks easy, but it's not so easy. You'd think it would be easy. It doesn't look like it's much. You've just got your three fingers covering the thumb and your other index fingers are just sort of at an angle and straight up. I love doing this for a longer period of time, because it reminds me of just pointing to God, pointing to the heavens. You are allowing yourself to just be one with that Divine Oneness. The **Suchi Mudra** is really good for your health, so you don't have to actually do it while you are meditating. But if you ever find yourself getting a little upset or a little cranky, or if you find yourself not being patient, do this mudra for a few minutes while you're breathing in through your nose, out through your mouth, your fingers are going up to God and it is a beautiful feeling. You'll feel very, very peaceful, very, very quickly. The Suchi Mudra.

Surya Mudra

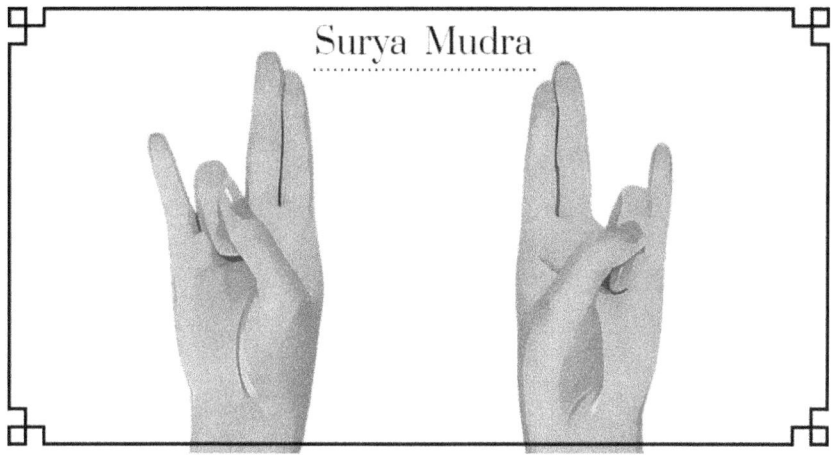

Mudra number seven is the **Surya Mudra**. This mudra, and I love this because it's a symbol of the sun and the sun is its own entity. The sun gives us life force. The sun gives us joy, it gives us plant life. It does so much. The sun is a beautiful, spiritual entity.

And so, the method is very simple. You just bend the ring finger and press it with the thumb and it actually helps sharpen the centre in your thyroid gland. But what it also does is it helps you to STOP THOUGHT and that is always the main goal. If you're going to do this one while you're meditating, well, I would suggest doing it for five minutes, but there are other ways that you can use this. You can go out, don't gaze right into the sun, but stand under the sun during the day of course, and it's a great blessing for you to do this, to honour the sun. You can bow to the sun and just say, *Thank you for the heat, the warmth, for giving us so much life force on this planet.* And you just thank the sun. And that's the Surya mudra.

Prana Mudra

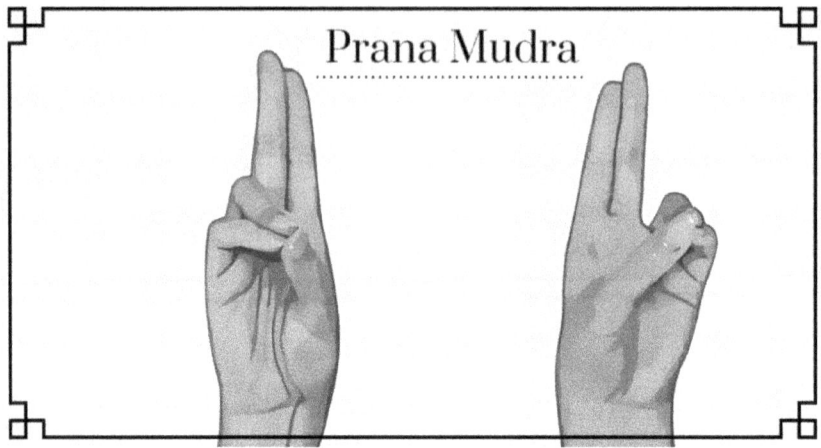

Oh, now everyone's going to love this one. This is the **Prana Mudra**, and of course, Prana means Life Force energy. So, this is the mudra of life. Now, it looks a little challenging, but it really is not challenging at all. You just bend your ring finger and little finger and touch the tips of those two fingers to the tip of the thumb keeping the remaining two fingers stretched, as you can see what our beautiful hand model is doing. And as it is the mudra of life, the Prana mudra is so great. It improves the power of life through you. You become much more active. You can become stronger in your conviction, and your personality, in a very calm way. And it is very, very, very beautiful. One can practice it at any time.

Apana Mudra

I think all of these mudras are great for improving immunity. And, of course, again they are also to bless you with a quiet mind, with Stillness and Silence in your mind. And here we have our final mudra, the **Apana Mudra**. Now, this is a very simple mudra to perform and you've probably seen it a lot. Maybe people don't realize when they're going to rock concerts that they're actually doing the Apana mudra. Yeah, rock on. It's very simple to do. As you can see our beautiful hand model doing, you just touch the two middle fingers to the tip of the thumb, stretch out your little finger and your index finger as straight as you can, or out to the sides a bit if you can. And you can either put your hand out doing it or put it up. And it is a mudra that is very, very beautiful because it is a gesture.

It's a really sacred hand gesture or what the Buddhists will call a seal used during meditation practice as a means of channelling the flow of the Kundalini, yet again, the flow of the Life Force of Prana, Apana.

So, there you have it, my friends. That's nine beautiful mudras that you can absolutely take advantage of to improve your health and life force and to still your mind. If you want to go deeper into learning more about mudras, there are many great books that go into great detail that you can find online, but I would recommend that you get the Buddhist explanation of these mudras because then you get the spiritual side of their True Purpose. There are other health benefits. People will go into that in great detail in these more detailed books. However, the main thing for us in practicing Sacred Mudras is to Awaken and for our meditation practice to go deeper. I'd like to thank the hand model very, very much for her beautiful hands today. Have fun with your mudras and know that you are so loved.

Write Down Your Realizations And Insights From Mudras

Laughing

Laughing Stops Thought

Laughing is something that science has been able to prove that leads to fast healing. As you all know I do whatever it takes to make people laugh. I mean, the moment I get to talk to all you guys, I'm laughing straight away. Not at you, just with you. Because when you are laughing, you're in a state of meditation, you're actually in the moment. There's no left brain activity or right brain activity. It's just that in that moment of pure, natural laughter we have no thought. It's just, *That's funny.* And so, whatever it takes, if you've got anyone in your life you feel is depressed, the highest thing to do is to make them laugh. And if someone can't laugh, get them to watch candid camera, or watch people slip on banana skins, which I don't find funny, but some people do. Monty Python's Silly Walk is hysterical!

I think most things are funny or I find something funny about them. You just watch things that uplift you, that make you laugh, because then that really helps heal and it's just so important.

Watching babies laugh is always great. That's why I recorded years ago The Laughing Meditation Program because people would just hear people laughing their arses off. We had all these little kids laughing. And then when I had the adults in the studio, if they didn't sound like they were laughing sincerely, I'd be like, *Okay, who ate the baked beans? I can smell your farts.* And everyone would start laughing in the studio.

I had all these funny signs ready. I don't know what it is about talking about farting, but it genuinely makes kids laugh a lot.

Anyway, I like watching behind-the-scenes of certain movies. In the Johnny Depp movie *Finding Neverland*, the kids that were in it all fell in love with Johnny Depp because he was Peter Pan to them. But in the movie, there was a scene at a dinner table with his wife and mother-in-law, where these other people were very, very serious and not laughing at all. While the adults aren't looking, Johnny Depp puts a spoon on his nose and the kids are supposed to laugh spontaneously. But it was challenging to do that scene because of the fact that they're going to film Johnny doing it first and then they've got to film the kids' faces when there's nothing to laugh at.

So, what Johnny Depp did was he brought in a whoopie cushion. So, that every time they had to laugh, he would sit on the whoopie cushion, and then all the kids would laugh. And the adults that were in it said it was so hard for them because they were supposed to remain really, really serious. And they said, there's nothing funnier than listening to a whoopie cushion.

You all know what a whoopie cushion is, right? Yes. It's a nicer way of saying a farting cushion, but you're just saying it's a whoopie cushion. Happiness heals. It totally heals.

And it's really interesting too, that scientists have been looking into meditation quite seriously in the past two decades. They are experimenting putting different sensors on the brain during meditation. And I've got this Fitbit. And so, for amusement, I'll go into meditation and the Fitbit shows that the heart rate goes down really fast because there's no stress in meditation. And it's really interesting that we talk about the left brain and the right brain, and people used to say, *Oh, that's absolute BS, Woo, Woo talk!* Now they're saying, *Oh yes, it's really true.*

When the left brain is totally functioning, it's taking you down rabbit holes, it's got all these thoughts going, bam, bam, bam, bam, bam. And when you practice meditation, you are turning off that left brain and you're actually eventually turning off the right brain as well. The left side of the brain is where there are all those thoughts.

And so that's the other way of becoming completely blissful and happy without having to laugh your arse off, is you go into that deep meditation where you experience bliss, you experience what it's like to be in Nirvana. And while that's happening, it improves your health so that you won't be constipated and you can do that very uplifting experience lovingly called farting. Us Aussies love a good farting joke and toilet humour. Well, we were all originally convicts after all!

Write Down Your Realizations And Insights From Laughing

Diet And Exercise

You Are Strong And You Are Beautiful

Diet

When you're eating protein like steak or chicken (always grass-fed), you want to always remember to thank that particular animal that they have now become part of your Enlightenment. *Thank You. For you are now part of my Enlightenment.* You just thank it sincerely rather than just eating it, because it has given up its life for you. So don't feel bad about it.

Don't all become vegan unless you want to. I used to be vegan and then I was a vegetarian for most of my life until I met my Teacher, Kundalini. She said I was going to absolutely energetically fade into nothingness. And I was very, very slim at the time. She said because I didn't eat meat that's why I was nearly passing out all the time from the energy. So, because she told me to start eating meat, I did. But still, I'd only have a steak, like two little bites. It did however give me my strength back because the Shakti coming from my Teacher was so strong and I could feel it all so I was very giddy and faint until I began to eat some salmon and chicken. I would eat a wee bit of steak occasionally but not very often.

When we buy our fruit and veggies, send them love and appreciation. At the grocery store, I'll see this beautiful lettuce that's so full of Prana. I will say to it in my heart and mind, *Oh, I love you so much. Look at you. Can I take you home?* And when we buy food, we want to feel the energy of the food. You know what I'm talking about? And please, if you can, buy organic and feel, when you go into a grocery store, the Pranic energy of certain fruit and veggies. You all know you can.

It's just amazing, it's so beautiful. It really is a beautiful tomato. Goodness me. My tomatoes are the best. They're so sweet. And then I just thank it. *Thank you so much. You are beautiful. Thank you for being part of my body and just thank you. Thank you for your nutrition. Thank you for your Life Force.* You just thank it. Love your fruit and veggies that you've got right now. Love this grapefruit, which you can eat straight away, because I'm giving it so much Love. And wherever you can, whether it's butter lettuce or whatever it is, anything that's in a container, write the words I love you. I love you, I love you.

And there you go. Pretty simple, but do it with all food. But particularly do it with protein, with meat, chicken, seafood, or whatever it is. Thank that animal for being part of your Enlightenment now and your nutrition. And then it's an incredible experience where the soul of that animal will be felt. It sounds weird, I know, but it's true. That was a living creature and you are now having that protein to assist your health. And so, you thank it greatly. It's a beautiful thing, then it is part of your life. Your Life Force.

Water

Water, water, water. It's so easy for you to just get in the habit of thanking your water every time you have a drink of water, or when you're in the shower. I bow at the end of my shower every time, and I'm bowing to the water to thank it for cleansing my body and for being there because it's been through hell and back going through all those pipes. And it's just incredible that we are made of so much water and we are not acknowledging water. Because when you're acknowledging water, you're acknowledging yourself as well. You're loving yourself. If you want to, you could even write on your water bottles. You can put, I love you. Thank you, thank you. I love you.

Because you are one with the water, and your intention is just to thank it and love it. You don't have to get all gushy and really feel it. You just have to say it and write it on the container, the water bottle, the milk bottle, anything. Write I love you, thank you. I mean, even on the top of a strawberry packet on the plastic, I'll put Thank you so much. I love you. To the strawberries. So, they're sitting in the fridge going, oh, thank you, yummy. And you just absolutely love it. And when you do that, it's incredible how much more hydrated you'll become. Because the brain, when you feel thirsty, that means you're very dehydrated. Very. So there is no time that you should really feel thirsty. So just keep drinking lots and lots of water and love your water. Everyone drink up. Cheers.

Exercise

You want to be as healthy as you can possibly be, and as strong as you can possibly be. You want your abs to be strong so that you can sit up and meditate for longer periods and keep yourself hydrated as much as you can because otherwise, it's really just such a challenge if you don't do this.

You want to live a long life, a healthy life overflowing with vitality and Divine Life Force Energy. Then when you become Enlightened you will be able to handle the full-on, strong Divine Energy that will be vibrating throughout... well everything! To awaken, to become Enlightened, is your Divine Purpose for being born. You will want to experience that Enlightenment for as many years as you can while you're still in the body.

Make sure that you've got a healthy body. Begin right now today. Do your eight deep breaths every hour, drink lots of lovely yummy water, and exercise.

The brain function is extremely important to your thyroid, to everything, because the thyroid definitely becomes stimulated from the Kundalini Awakening. So, we must have a healthy thyroid.

Write Down Your Realizations And Insights From Diet And Exercise

Praying For Others Raises Our Own Consciousness
Prayer Is A Gift To Give And To Receive

When we pray for others, we are praying for ourselves, but we're not doing it to pray for ourselves. Because we are all one. It is so beautiful to pray for others, have compassion for others, and feel it so strongly in our heart. And that is how I became fully Enlightened. My friend Ian Miller, an amazing Australian guitarist and my best friend for many years, left the body after years of battling cancer. I played with him for years. He's one of the songwriters and was in John Paul Young's band for years. He was on a poster on my wall when I was a teenager, and when I grew up I actually got to write songs and play with him for over four years. *Talk about visualization working.* I thought he was so beautiful when I was a teenager and I ended up working with him and writing songs with him. So, whatever you look at, you end up attracting into your life, even a pop star guitarist.

After he'd just left the body, I had his photograph and I just looked at it, sent Light to it, and lit a candle. And then I started reading *The Tibetan Book of the Living and Dying*. But I didn't like all of the exercises in that book so I just stayed with the exercises that I felt aligned with. If something in the book didn't feel right to my heart I would go back to the ones that opened my heart. I kept speaking to his spirit saying, *You are surrounded by this Light and you are reborn into the most amazing, miraculous place.* I didn't know if he needed to be reborn here or go to a heaven plane, or if he was Enlightened as he went through the Stargate. Anyway, I did that for nine days keeping a candle going throughout the nine days. I made a shrine for him and after the nine days I tore up the photograph, I burnt it, and then I said, *Now you are dissolved into Eternity forever.* And then I planted a rose bush and put the ashes of the photograph into the ground with the rose bush.

And that was when I had my first experience of going through the Stargate. And I spoke to an Enlightened friend of mine named Jeff because this was a few months before my full Enlightenment, and I shared my experience of Ian with Jeff. I told Jeff what had happened, and I told him about Ian, and he said, *Well, that's the way it works when you start praying for others. They actually end up helping you because we are all one.* Since then I have never stopped from that moment onwards praying for others, because it's the most beautiful experience. And there's so many different ways to pray for others. After my awakening I began experimenting on different ways to pray for others and then I got the download for the Golden Ballroom Visualization. And then not long after that, I got the download on how to transmit this Light to others so that they can transmit it to others.

Every time you receive a Light Transmission, the things in your body, the things in your life that could have happened horribly, won't happen because you are so God-Governed. It's a miraculous thing. And when I started realizing and seeing the differences in my consciousness the longer I was with Kundalini as my Teacher, the more I would just almost dissolve into a puddle every time I saw her. My gratitude was so immense, and it still is every day of my life.

I am so grateful for, and to, Kundalini, as I would love for you all to also be because you would not be here today, experiencing a better life, if it was not for her.

Write Down Your Realizations And Insights From Praying For Others Raises Our Own Consciousness

What Is Prayer

Prayer Is Miraculous

What is prayer? Do any of you presently pray? When you do pray, who do you think you're praying to? Seriously, when you pray, where is your consciousness? Do you think you're praying to a God that's separate to you? No, you don't. You really don't. Because duality isn't the way to pray. There's no duality. You're not begging someone or something. Your Diamond, your Higher Self, is Omnipotent Power. It is the Creator, Eternity, whatever you choose to call it, God, Love. It created you for goodness sake.

It is omnipresent. That means your consciousness is actually omnipresent and one day you will experience that if you haven't already. And it's incredible to experience omnipresence. And it's omniscient. That means all wisdom, all that ever was, is, or will be known in all dimensions is known by the Divine, and you have the Divine. The Divine is animating your very being. You couldn't breathe without the Divine. You don't wake up every 5 minutes when you're sleeping, *Oh, am I breathing? Is my heart still beating?* Or maybe some of you do.

You trust that you breathe, and that your heart is working, even though you may not yet be able to go internally into your body. Eventually, you will. Some of you may have already. You can just feel safe that the body has been made perfectly as long as we look after this blessing called a body. As long as we exercise and we eat well and we bless our food and do all that great, spiritual food for the soul.

And especially water, drink lots of water. Well then, you stay young forever. Well, you feel like you stay young forever. I sure do. And it's just a magical way to live because you're happy. It's not even the word happy. It is joy. The only way I can describe this hum that is there 24/7 is – it's joy and peace combined in stillness.

And it's amusing. Life is amusing. You can always find irreverent things, which I always love. That's why I adore Monty Python. Who doesn't? Silly walk, anyone? My Favourite Monty Python movie is The Life of Brian. It just cracks me up. *I'm not the Messiah. I'm not. You are the Messiah you are!! OK, You're not the Messiah. OK, I am the Messiah. You're the Messiah. Praise The Messiah called Brian!*

I always think of Swami Muktananda, if you've read his book, *Play Of Consciousness*, when his master gives him his sandals, and he won't wear them on his feet. He just puts them on his head in great reverence. He can't believe he's getting his master's footwear. For some reason that happened in *The Life of Brian*. I'm not spoiling it. You can't spoil it. You can't watch it enough, actually. And someone said that you put the sandals on your head and so everyone who were after Brian thought Brian was the Messiah because they'd all be walking around with their sandals on the top of their head.

So, then I think of Swami Muktananda. Anyway, it's a great movie. Those guys were brilliant. Some of them are still with us, but they're absolutely brilliant.

OK. So, when we pray, we're not praying to some outside force. Even if you think it is, it is the Divine that created every cell of your being. Like the Bible says, God knows every hair on your head. And it's true. When I'm transmitting Light to someone, even if I don't have their photograph, it doesn't matter where they are in the world, it's omnipresent. Consciousness is omnipresent, and because everything is consciousness, therefore can you see how you are omnipresent, now?

Because you can think of someone, and pray for that person, and they can be on the other side of the world, and they will feel it. Maybe they won't feel it consciously, however, something good's going to happen. Or something that could have been bad won't happen to them which happens a lot.

When your Diamond is clear that means when you're praying, you are praying through this omnipotent, omnipresent, omniscient Creator, Eternity, that can do anything. So, you're not doing it per se. I don't want to get into duality either, but your intention is used along with your consciousness by Your Higher Self, your Divine. When that Diamond become clear you become a beautiful conduit for the Light.

www.MyDivineDiamond.com

It's not, *Oh, Michele healed me.* No, her *Enlightenment that goes through her, her clarity, her Diamond and her intention of prayer healed me.* Some others will say, *It is just a coincidence that my life is better.* I say, *Well, that's not a coincidence, remember. A lot of Light, Effort, and Love went into you.* Of course, I never say that to anyone. It matters not to me to ever be acknowledged, it is all God.

That is such a beautiful thing that we are going to be able to pray for people that you love, or a country, or anything, and teach about the ways to do that and go through these blessed practices today. Prayer is not begging. It's not a, *Look, God, really. If you do this, I promise I will stop eating pizza.* I don't know what people do when they say stuff like that. But the paradox here is if someone is sincerely praying for help – maybe someone they love is in the hospital – when someone is sincerely praying for help, I can feel it. And it's like the Angels or the Enlightened ones, we all feel it, and so we immediately pray by going into Silence.

I always love to pray for those people who are sincerely asking for help, even if they're begging, because of love. Even if it's desperation or they just don't know what else to do. If you say, *God, help me,* and it's sincere, then that is a very good prayer. It's just that when you're trying to do a trade-off, that's not prayer. It's not begging. You don't have to beg for God. In fact, your Higher Self has gone before you and prepared the way. What is it that you want? Just give thanks for it immediately. *Thank you for that. Yay, you Rock, God*! It's a Divine Knowing almost a command to this Divine Energy.

You can't be nasty to the Light. There's no good or bad in the Light, there's just Love and, *What do you want? I'll give it to you.* And that's why it's good, when we do our prayers and intentions and affirmations, to say you already have it. *I have that thing and I'm grateful. So grateful!* Because the subconscious mind only knows now because there is only now. You are living in timelessness. In fact, time is an illusion that was created by man because it was just easier at the time. It's like money. It was created so that you didn't have to put the big sheep over your shoulder. *Can I have some flour please? I'll do a swap for it with this sheep.*

It is a privilege to pray. Always remember to pray for others as well as yourself. Receive and give, remember? Be open to receive and give. So, that's why listening to the affirmation music or going through the Manifestation Video Book or any of our products, it's all affirmations and wonderful K.I.S.S. (Keep It Simple and Spiritual) explanations of how this world works.

When someone is attempting to teach you in a way that says, *I'm high and mighty and you're not,* and, *I don't know if you're going to understand this. But maybe I'll initiate you if you're lucky. If you pay me a zillion dollars.* It's simple. God, the Divine, omnipresence, is forever, always has been, always will be, and is all loving.

There's not a mind like a person has in the Divine. It is pure creative power. And you have to direct that power where you want it to go. You can feel it when you're directing that power in a loving way, but a strong way. Not like a wimpy, *Please, please Mr. Please!*

Another thing is energy transference is not good prayer. I studied everything because I was curious. I wanted to know this thing called God, the Divine, so I could feel how that would work. And then I started studying the ancient Buddhist ways of teaching the monks. It was similar to Reiki. They envision a pattern in their head to still their mind so that they can be a conduit of the Divine. But if they put their hands on you, and they've got negativity in them, when someone is doing Reiki or hands-on healing you're going to take on that negativity. There are very good Reiki professionals, and they know how to NOT transfer their energy to you, however, you don't want Reiki if you don't know who the person is as they may not know what they are doing and then you can take on their energy which may be quite yukky. Plus, you are also giving them your energy. A sticky business.

You don't need to be next to the person. They don't need to know you're praying for them. You don't even have to have their photograph. You have to get out of the way and know it's not you praying, it's your love and intention to be used as a conduit for the Divine. Which is the same Divine in you, in me, and in everyone else. It's just that many people's Divine is blocked and they can't feel it.

A lot of people's intuition isn't Intuition. It's just, *Which way will I go? Left or right? I don't know.* Whereas Intuition, when you have a clear diamond, you are directed. Always. The right Divine way. The right Divine action will be taken.

And that way you know your karma has been burnt away. Because there's no such thing as good karma, there's only bad karma. Because it's interesting, I know I've talked about karma before, but people don't get it. I didn't get it until I was awake. I thought, *People are saying they've got good karma. It's all crap. None of it's good.* You just want to burn it away because karma is all the experiences that's been sitting on your Diamond lifetime after lifetime. And you want to burn that away.

So, if you want to look at it in a different way, good karma means less karma. Simple as that. That is why I do visualizations with you guys. The Golden Ballroom, the different things that have been downloaded to me, the waterfall to clear you, and to make you feel better. I do these because as I'm sending the Light to you, as I'm speaking to you, it is always working for you.

Write Down Your Realizations And Insights From What Is Prayer

Simple Prayers To Uplift Loved Ones

*Assist Your Loved Ones Through
The Power Of Prayer*

And now in the Silence, write down the name of the person you are praying for. If you do know what the person looks like, I want you to visualize them happy and laughing and Light just glowing from them. And then after you visualize that for a little while, just feel the expanse of Love within you, Love for this person, Love for the Eternal. Just do what you can to hear that hum of Love, because that will heal everything and everyone. See them now, laughing, giggling, healthy, vital. And if you don't know what they look like, just know that they are laughing and giggling and every cell of their being is giggling with love and health and vitality. And now just quietly say as you inwardly bow to them, *The Divine Presence is with you and has gone before you to prepare the way and you are loved. You are 100% God- Governed.*

It's important to get into that stillness within you because then your words penetrate through the veil and reach the Divine Presence in that person, in that stillness. See, it doesn't take long because the Divine has already done it, that intention, as soon as you wrote their name down. But when you add a prayer, some people say to pray for others, to just be in the stillness. But for me, I do every trick in the book so I also visualize them happy. When I've got your photograph, of course, I use that. You do a prayer for them, you're speaking to their Divine Presence and they feel it. We are all one. That diamond is your diamond that's in that person. It may be clogged more than other people, but they feel it. And if you know them, they're probably calling you right now.

So, this is how prayer works. Prayer is visualizing someone really happy. And prayer is also giving of yourself wherever you can. I always tithe to my Spiritual Source and I also always tithe to the Salvation Army, and to the Red Cross to help animals. If you have $10, you tithe a dollar. I can't tell you how quickly it comes back to you when you're tithing for love. When you dislike someone, you tithe in their name and whatever disharmony was there evaporates. They NEVER ever need to know. Always do it anonymously when you can. This is for your peace of mind because it is very unhealthy to dislike people. If you have some sort of grudge or there's someone in your family, who might've left the body already, you can still tithe in their name and experience a healing. Whenever you go to the Salvation Army or the Red Cross online they have a section asking if you like this tithe to be dedicated to somebody's memory. When you tithe in someone's name, it's like they're the ones that have tithed and they get blessed regardless of whether they're in a new body or not. Tithing in someone's name assists them greatly. I do it for my grandparents. I always do it for Ian, for Wilma McIntyre, for people that I know that have left the body, I always tithe in their name.

It's really, really good to never tithe in your own name and to do it for somebody else. You are blessing that person greatly, whether you're doing it because you like them, or you dislike them, or you love them. It is like they've done it because we're all one. We're part of the tapestry of Light. So the more we do this, the less we're about ourselves. When I tithe to my Teacher I do not say this is in someone's name I just press send on PayPal and silently say this is for …… Now I do a lot of prayer and I get you to do a lot of affirmations for yourself because it's very, very important that you become very independent and that you have your own money and success and opportunities in your life so that you don't have to think about that human crapola, so that you can think about other people and get on with living fully. Let go of all the small petty stuff.

Otherwise, everybody gets too into *me, me, me, me, me* too much. And it's important to love the body. It is good for you to not think of your body as yourself, but as the Divine in this vehicle. You wash and polish your car, don't you? Well, this is you washing and polishing the cells of your body, of your car. You're not attached to it, but you love it.

Write Down Your Realizations And Insights From Simple Prayers To Uplift Loved Ones

Mindfulness

Awareness Is Key To Your Enlightenment

Mindfulness is Awareness. If you're aware of your thoughts, then it can be very powerful to release the thoughts that are holding you down. However, most people are not even aware of their own thoughts. Because most people are so immersed in the rabbit hole of thoughts, they are not aware of what has happened in their lives and they don't realize they are in fact the one who is creating their reality.

Alright. Now I will share with you how I was able to bear witness and to be able to just see the consciousness, the thoughts, without being affected. And if there's even a slight reaction to a thought there is fear behind that thought. Most of the time a totally irrational fear but fear nonetheless. We must look into that fear for it to be dissolved and find out what's going on, which is an empowering thing to do.

A friend of mine was going through a similar thing, and she's becoming very aware of when she feels like there's a victim mentality.

So, I said to her there's nothing in your life where you are a victim. You have a beautiful family, a husband who adores you who is a very spiritual man, beautiful children, a great job, purpose, lots of different things. I said it's just a remnant from a past life that attempts to make you reactionary to certain situations, but they don't exist anymore.

One of the things you can do when a random thought comes up is to just stop and say, *Okay, well I know that's not the truth. I know it's not the truth because look at my life, look at those who love me. I have Light sent to me every day. So, I know that is just a remnant. It's a shadow from a past life. It's not the truth. It's just not the truth.* Then you are clear and shinier.

Even if someone is being nasty, you won't be reactionary because we cannot take anything personally. It's very, very challenging to understand that when certain things happen in our life, and it feels really personal, it's not. It's the maya. It's just blowing farts in the wind. They may smell but this too shall pass. You just want a gentle breeze at your back. You don't want it just taking you anywhere down which road it wants to take you because it's going to be random. Because the maya isn't intelligent. It's not wisdom, it's just random rabbit hole crapola.

I made a decision one day. I was not told to do this. I just made a decision one day many years ago. I just decided I'm going to have a day as often as possible where I stop every single thought, every thought that comes up, unless I'm actually working, writing a book, or something like that. Because it's very, very challenging to stop your thought when you are not awake yet and you're actually working on a project.

What I did was, every thought that would come in, I would say in my mind, I wouldn't say it out loud, *You are not real.* I wouldn't let it take me to the ice cream store, to the Indian food shop, nothing. I would just say, *You are not real. You are not real.* I wouldn't watch any movies. I would allow myself to read spiritual books. And at that stage, I was just reading Swami Muktananda's Play of Consciousness so many times a month. It was ridiculous. I couldn't put the thing down. It's just so awesome. And you get so much Shakti from it, you can feel it.

So, *You're not real. You're not real.* Sometimes it would feel like thousands of times in a day. *You're not real. You are not my thought.* I wouldn't let it tell me anything. *You are not real. No, not real.* After a few months of doing this at least one day a week, I could sometimes have a silent mind up to an hour of no thought. And I didn't notice until one day I was going for a nice long walk gazing up at all the nice electric lights. And I realized I'd been on that long walk and had not had one thought, nothing. *Who's that person walking over there? Where are they from? Oh, I wonder if they've got a car*. Nothing.

I cannot estimate or emphasize how greatly this assisted me in experiencing such peace of mind and, of course, more and more Light. When you really, really, really wish to be in the moment, you have to use your willpower and your self-discipline.

Back in the old days, I used to do this as well, but only if a negative thought came up. But at this stage, I wasn't really a person who experienced negative thoughts, not really. Maybe a tiny little one here and there, but I just didn't want any thought. So I used to say, *STOP,* back in the day if I had a negative thought, *Just stop. It's not the truth. It's not the truth.* But then when I met my Teacher, Kundalini, who said, *It's all about no thought at all.* And she taught us that when thought came up, she would just say, OM MANI PADME HUM.

And then I said, *I don't even want to do that for this day, this one day a week.* And then I would make it two days a week and three days a week. Or, *Okay, I'll work with Treavor in the morning and then in the afternoon and all evening I will either be in meditation or no thought.* And it was then when my meditations became deeper and deeper so I could go into stillness fast and experience many Divine flashes. This is just before the Stargate happened.

I had those flashes all the time where it's the beginning of the Stargate because there's no thought. You are allowing thought to be released, and you are less blocked, because it just blocks everything, all those thoughts. So it's not easy, but it's fun. I can't even tell you why it's fun, even though it's not easy. I wasn't doing it because I thought that I would be Enlightened. I truly never had the thought that I could become Enlightened but obviously, my Consciousness in that miraculous Kundalini Energy knew better. I just loved my Teacher and Loved God!

That thought never really entered my head that I would be like my Teacher, ever. I don't know why. It just didn't. I just wanted to go really deep in being in Union with God. I didn't know that all of this stuff would happen to me. That's why it's good not to have a destination, and to know that you are already there. You are already in Enlightenment because Enlightenment is everything. It's Truth. Those of you who have had a prayer CD from me, you'll hear me say that. I've said it on every single one of them. Enlightenment is my truth. My truth is Enlightenment. Enlightenment is here and Enlightenment is everywhere. So, if Enlightenment is everywhere, you are Enlightened. It's just that your Diamond requires a shine up to unblock your consciousness, that's all. And having thought stop, stopping in the name of love, is what it's all about. Yes. Let us all Stop Thought and Dive Into The Ocean Of Eternal Life. You Are Immortal Consciousness and You Are So Very Loved.

Write Down Your Realizations And Insights From Mindfulness

A Desire To Awaken The Mystical Experience

Millions of people right now are experiencing a yearning and desire to awaken to their unique gifts and offer them in service to the world — while living a life of joy and fulfilment. It's a surging of the Enlightenment of spirit, that is your truth, a virtual global awakening, on a scale never observed before.

The Truth is 99% of the people born on this beautiful planet have waited a long time to have this experience. An opportunity, to awaken to their Divine Consciousness.

Why do people love the sight of Light Shows, gold, diamonds, and rare gems? Why are we so mesmerized by Fireworks and Light Shows? It unconsciously reminds us of the Light and the experience of Divine Dimensions. Of going through the Divine Stargate.

It is the Divine's way of giving us a taste of where we really live in consciousness when we are awake. Everyone wants to be there and come home. OM. I always thought it was only saints and old gray-haired or bald-headed Holy men who could be Enlightened.

That is not the Truth EVERYONE can become Free. I know this because I have become free and now I dedicate my life to others becoming free, and also enjoying their journey towards freedom through teaching how they can become more successful and happier right now. Happier in every area of their life starting with their soul. Join people from all over the globe and experience for yourself how far you can go. It is unlimited.
www.MicheleBlood.com/Gold

Here Is What Others Are Saying About The Mystical Experience

"The most amazing thing about it is that when you connect to this energy to help someone you are really raising your own connection and consciousness so fast. I am growing in vibration and feeling alive inside."
- *William, Mystical Experience Member*

"Dearest Angel, Michele I had, after your Transmission and Prayer, a very fast miracle. A transfer to Kochin City came in 20 hours. It's incredibly beautiful. It has to be felt to be believed. I am grateful for your kind blessed light. It has improved my health also. Thanking your beautiful soul."
- *Sreekanth, Mystical Experience Member*

"Since joining I continue to live each day with much more joy and happiness. I feel like I am being reborn and my consciousness is awakening."
- *Gary, Mystical Experience Member*

"The Mystical Advancement & Success Event has instantaneously and profoundly changed my life for the better-and I am so grateful. I am so grateful to the Divine through Michele, which has awakened that within me, and brought forth graces I had never conceived of."
- *Nicole, Mystical Experience Member*

"I experienced the profound awareness of 'There is only NOW' and everything is an illusion except Enlightenment. Nothing else is real. Thank you for the Light Transmissions with the Divine through you."
- *Susanne, Texas*

Resources

To sign up for Light Transmissions to bring more Prosperity, Success, Beauty, and Divine Harmony to your Beautiful Life go to:
www.ReceiveDivineLight.com

To purchase the Visualizations I talk about like *The Golden Ballroom* and *The Pool Of Enlightened Samadhi* as well as many positive books and affirmation music albums go to:
www.MagnetToSuccess.com

For all of my Positive Music videos and videos to assist you to transform fast for you to experience deep happiness, oneness, and success go to:
www.YouTube.com/MicheleBlood

The World's First Manifestation Video Book
Manifestation Through The Power Of Mysticism also available as an app on your iPhone.
www.ManifestationVideoBook.com

The Most Anticipated Prosperity App Is At Last Here! You Can Be A Magnet To Money! Go to:
www.MagnetToMoneyApp.com

The FREE Affirmation Power App. Your ultimate tool for daily affirmations, manifestation techniques, and transformative content!
www.AffirmationPowerApp.com

Notes

Notes

Notes

Notes

Notes

Notes

www.ingramcontent.com/pod-product-compliance
Lightning Source LLC
Chambersburg PA
CBHW071659090426
42738CB00009B/1590